The Team America Loves to Hate

THE TEAM AMERICA LOVES TO HATE

Why Baseball Fans Despise the New York Yankees

Charles R. Warner

PRAEGER
An Imprint of ABC-CLIO, LLC

A B C **≋** C L I O

Santa Barbara, California • Denver, Colorado • Oxford, England

Library of Congress Cataloging-in-Publication Data

Warner, Charles R.
  The team America loves to hate : why baseball fans despise the New York Yankees /
Charles R. Warner.
    p. cm.
  Includes bibliographical references and index.
    ISBN 978-0-313-35704-6 (alk. paper) — ISBN 978-0-313-35705-3
(ebook : alk. paper)
1. New York Yankees (Baseball team)   2. Sports spectators—Psychology.   3. Sports
spectators—Attitudes.   I. Title.
  GV875.N4W386   2009
  796.357'64097471—dc22   2009030409

13   12   11   10   09   1   2   3   4   5

This book is also available on the World Wide Web as an eBook.
Visit www.abc-clio.com for details.

ABC-CLIO, LLC
130 Cremona Drive, P.O. Box 1911
Santa Barbara, California 93116-1911

This book is printed on acid-free paper ∞
Manufactured in the United States of America

CONTENTS

PREFACE

For some, the title of this book might convey the impression that my desire is to hear the world respond resoundingly in the affirmative; to raise its collective voice in a passionate declaration of antipathy toward that most storied team in Major League Baseball. Not so. While I have always been reasonably confident that a significant number of baseball fans harbor significant antipathy for the New York Yankees, confirming to some degree that this is the case does not constitute the fulfillment of some personal wish. It's just the way things are, and even if things weren't that way, it is certainly not my intention in writing this book to shepherd that hatred into existence. In other words, this is not a "how to" manual inspired by my evangelical zeal to unite humankind through malevolence toward a professional sports franchise. It's merely an investigation of a preexisting condition, an attempt to more fully understand a current reality, rather than to proselytize for what I might consider a new and improved one. For these reasons, I have chosen to allow this book to be driven by the opinions of fans that self-identify as Yankee haters, using those opinions as the raw materials from which I attempt to construct a coherent explanation of this mass phenomenon. I do so hoping that this effort will be received in the spirit it is offered; with a recognition that even high-stakes hardball should be an enjoyable diversion from more serious matters, and that such diversions become even more enjoyable when they receive a bit of serious consideration. That said, a few observations should be made regarding the general treatment of the many e-mailed fan narratives found in these pages.

First, it should be noted that the form and content of these fan narratives tend to reflect the significant intellectual and cultural diversity that characterizes baseball fandom itself. Achieving the degree of formal consistency necessary for the presentation of these diverse expressions in a single document was, to say the least, a daunting task. In all cases, my goal was to achieve readability without jeopardizing the intended meaning or affective charge of the fan's message, guided by the imperative of keeping changes to a minimum. For instance, in utilizing the medium of e-mail, one characterized by immediacy, efficiency, and a lack of formal editing, I often felt the need to modify grammar, spelling, and punctuation in the interest of presenting information coherently. Fans often lapse into a type of shorthand peppered with abbreviations and slang when engaged in e-mail exchanges, taking advantage of the reservoir of common references and terminology shared by like-minded fans. Because the readers of this book may not all have easy access to this insider's lexicon, I have sometimes taken the liberty of replacing unfamiliar slang with Standard English, and abbreviations with full phrasing, when it seemed necessary. When fans refer to teams, players, stadiums, or events by using partial or colloquial nicknames, I often embellish such references to ensure comprehension by a more general readership. Fans whose messages are cited are identified only by the usernames they have provided in order to create an account for the use of message boards on Major League Baseball team Web sites. In order to preserve the integrity and creativity associated with these usernames, the only change I have made to any of them is the capitalization of the first letter in the name, as required for compliance to style guidelines. Creative modifications to the term "Yankees" was also a prevalent occurrence in these fan narratives, resulting in a variety of comic mutations: "Spankees," "Yankmees," "Spankmees," "Stankees," and so forth. As these variants seem easily decoded by the average reader, I felt no need to correct such references. Indeed, they're just too colorful—and meaningful—to correct.

While authoring a book tends to be a solitary endeavor, thanks must go out to a number of individuals and institutions for their support, encouragement, and inspiration. First, I'd like to express my gratitude to East Stroudsburg University of Pennsylvania, particularly the University-Wide Sabbatical Leave Committee, for granting my request for sabbatical leave for the purpose of writing this book. While some of my faculty colleagues have managed to compose book-length works while performing all of the daily duties enumerated in their job descriptions, I now look upon those folks with an awe borne of the knowledge that there's no way I could have successfully kept all those balls in the air. I am truly grateful for the opportunity to pursue this project with the singular focus that only a sabbatical leave could provide. Many thanks go out to my colleagues in ESU's Department of Communication Studies, who have supported my efforts by graciously accommodating my absence. I've missed you all and look forward to getting back in the swing of things. Thanks also go out to my students, many of whom provided valuable early feedback on this project by simply stopping by my office to talk baseball. Much credit is due to my wife and daughter, both of whom are Yankee fans; their tolerance for living under the same roof with someone who would write such a book is to be commended. Actually, I'm just thankful that they didn't murder me in my sleep. I owe a significant debt to my father for being my childhood exemplar of how to be a proper baseball fan (i.e., sitting on the couch, yelling at the television). I'd like to recognize the willingness of fan culture scholar Roger Aden to advise and encourage me, a complete stranger, during the preparatory stages of this project, as well as the willingness of my faculty colleague, Andrea McClanahan, to introduce us. Another faculty colleague, Patricia Kennedy, deserves my gratitude for offering insight on matters related to intellectual property in the age of online communication. Many thanks are due to the folks at Praeger Publishers for their receptive response to the idea that the phenomenon of Yankee hatred among baseball fans is worthy of examination.

Finally, my deepest gratitude goes out to all of the fans who had the time, energy, and inclination to respond when someone chose to ask the question, "Who hates the Yankees?" Obviously, without their contributions, this book could not exist.

Chapter 1

WHAT'S IT ALL ABOUT?

In the summer of 2006, as I was driving back home to Northeastern Pennsylvania from Pittsburgh, I began the mental recap of the weekend that had just transpired. It was the annual baseball weekend, a get-together with a few guys I went to graduate school with who can still stand to be in my company for a few days at a time. There's the requisite catching up on each other's lives, reminiscences about the old days, bad jokes, a few beers, and, of course, a couple of baseball games, which provide the excuse for all of this. The location is determined through a fairly simple geographical calculus; with the participants residing in Michigan, Cleveland, Columbus, and Northeastern Pennsylvania, the equalization of driving time toward a central location is one of the goals. If Major League Baseball is to be part of the mix, our destination is often a group of seats at an Indians weekend series. This tends to sit well with this crowd, as three of the four grew up in the Cleveland area as loyal Indians fans and remain so to this day (the fourth participant, a Cincinnati Reds fan, somehow manages to endure the indignity of hanging with us, mainly out of respect for the institution of majority rule). But even the most ardent Indians fan yearns to see how the other half roots, to experience a familiar ritual in a new context, and a quick glance at the road atlas yields an obvious conclusion: Pittsburgh is a no-brainer.

However, Pittsburgh's geographic centrality was only one plus among several resulting in this choice. First, the Pirates represented a neutral fan focus for the members of our group; in other words, none of us really cared if they won or lost. This portended less arguing about baseball and more time for beer. Second, the 2006 Pirates were a team with little hope of on-field success, which tends to make ticket availability a non-issue, and modest attendance tends to enhance the availability of stadium vendors which, in turn, enhances the availability of beer. Third, none of us had attended a game at PNC Park, an intimate gem of a stadium opened in 2001, which had quickly developed a reputation for not having a bad seat in the house. Finally, the weekend of our gathering featured a series pitting the Pirates against the San Francisco Giants, a team that featured one Barry Bonds, an outfielder who once played in Pittsburgh, before the allure of big-market money led him away from this small-market franchise. Seeing how his former fans reacted to his return to where it all began provided an irresistible sidebar to the game itself, supplying sufficient content for discussion to justify yet another round of beers.

On that drive home from Pittsburgh, all that beer was soon forgotten. But memories of the Bonds factor dominated my thoughts. His presence at the ballpark that weekend seemed to color every aspect of the experience, the first being our assumption regarding the easy availability of tickets. Indeed, both of the games we attended were virtual sellouts, and the seats we were able to secure served as proof that there really wasn't a bad seat in the house. The reaction of the Pittsburgh fans every time Bonds strode to the plate revealed why this was the toughest ticket in town. They simply hate this guy, and they showed up in droves at PNC Park not so much to cheer for the Pirates, but to jeer Bonds mercilessly. Their boos seemed to bring them more joy than the two Pirates victories, and Bonds's performance at the plate that weekend provided ample opportunity for booing. When Bonds took an errant two-strike swing so mighty that he landed on his backside while being called out, the entire stadium erupted into the most raucous cheer of the weekend (and, considering the Pirates' 2006 record, perhaps the entire season). As I drove through central Pennsylvania, I tried to make sense of it all. Why all this joy in hatred? I realize that Bonds is not widely perceived as the poster boy for clean living and good sportsmanship. But other than relieving the Pirates of his high-priced bat by going to another team, what had Barry Bonds done to them to deserve such acrimony? I mean, it's not as if he abandoned the Pirates to become a terrorist, or one of Satan's henchmen, or (worst of all) a member of the New York Yankees. Now *that* would motivate the hatred I had witnessed that weekend. As it happens, that's also what motivated the writing of this book.

For the remainder of my journey that day, thoughts of the specific hatred aimed at Barry Bonds by Pirates fans were eclipsed by what seems to be a far more commonplace phenomenon: Yankee hatred by baseball fans of every stripe other than pinstripes. I recalled a discussion with the man who was partially responsible for my move to Pennsylvania some 20 years ago and who was, at that time, serving as the chairperson of the academic department that offered me my first full-time faculty position. He had grown up in the small town where our university is located—a small borough in the Pocono Mountains, about 85 miles north of Philadelphia. By virtue of some mix of proximity, state pride, and reasonably clear radio reception, he had also grown up a Phillies fan. Like many of our discussions, this one eventually turned to the subject of baseball and, at some point, I uttered the word "Yankees." Now, this guy is impeccably mannered, highly rational, and one of the most diplomatically skilled people I've ever met. But the venom that spewed from his mouth at the mere mention of that word was not only a little shocking but, in some ways, inexplicable. First, he's a fan of the Philadelphia Phillies—a National League franchise with virtually no history of direct competition against the American League Yankees—so this animus couldn't derive from some on-field rivalry in which the Yankees crushed the fortunes of his team. True, the Poconos have become something of a bedroom community for New Yorkers seeking an escape from urban congestion and high taxation, and the Yankee fandom that accompanied this migration has proven an irritant to the Phillies faithful in the area. But this guy just doesn't seem that parochial in his attitudes. He fully appreciates New York's status as a cultural center, spends significant time in the city, and even attended graduate school at New York University. I mean, the guy has never even had a driver's license! How New York is that? But it's all trumped by Yankee hatred.

Searching my memory for a more explicable instance of Yankee hatred, I quickly settled on my own experience as a Cleveland Indians fan. One of my earliest baseball memories is of attending a game pitting the Indians against the Yankees, sometime in the 1960s. Actually, it is a set of memories, the first of which involves wondering why I was sitting behind a huge pole that obstructed my view of most of the playing field. Yes, these were the cheap seats at that horrific sports mausoleum known as Cleveland Municipal Stadium—a place where, more than 30 years after its construction, one could still detect the smell of wet concrete; where a simple trip to the men's room became a psyche-scarring ritual of dehumanization, centered around the edifice of an endless porcelain trough conceived prior to the notion that individual urinals might be a more dignified way to go; where the winds off Lake Erie would swirl around the interior of the cavernous structure, requiring fans to don jackets and sweaters on an otherwise sweltering July afternoon; where fans in the cheap seats sat behind steel columns that supported the leaking roof. These were minor inconveniences to a kid attending a Major League Baseball game, but I couldn't help wondering, "Do Yankee fans have to put up with this stuff?" Of course, they did have to endure similar indignities, at least until the remodeling of Yankee Stadium in the 1970s solved a similar pole problem in the Bronx. But in my youthful ignorance, my animosity toward all things Yankee took root.

To this day, I retain the artifactual evidence of another memory linked to the development of my own Yankee hatred—my "I Hate the Yankees Hankee." I can't recall if it was distributed as a promotional item at a game I attended, or if I came by it in some other way. But the fact that I still have it is a testament to the resilience of Yankee hatred among Indians fans like me. Featuring the Indians logo and a facsimile of the signature of Pete Franklin, a local sports talk radio personality in that era, the only other images on this white piece of cloth are the words "I Hate the Yankees Hankee" written in simple block letters. The obvious intent here was to have Indians fans wave them in unison when the Yankees threatened to score a run, thereby invoking some mystical juju that would paralyze the enemy and enhance the Indians' prospects for victory. But its greater value is as an icon of remembrance, signifying the innocent hope of my own childhood and, more importantly, fixing the identity of the hated other for all time. While most of us grew up to abandon fantasies of affecting the outcome of games through the sheer common will of the fan base, the residual Yankee hatred remains. What also remains is a nagging memory of *why* such promotional items were commonplace when the Yankees came to town. A series against the Yankees was a really big deal in Cleveland—so big that Major League Baseball often scheduled a home series against the Yankees on the July 4th weekend in order to boost the Indians' revenue stream by enticing a large holiday crowd with a marquee opponent. I know I should have been grateful for this tactic, designed as it was to assist a struggling, small-market franchise. Instead, I resented the notion that the Indians needed this sort of charity from the likes of the Yankees in order to survive. Indeed, I would have rather seen the Tribe move to New Orleans or Miami than suffer the indignity of this New York-style noblesse oblige.

Now, that kind of attitude is just crazy. It's completely irrational. It's entirely self-defeating. But when it comes to the Yankees, it's an attitude that I share with countless baseball fans. So, what is it about baseball fans that leads them to harbor such loathing for just another baseball team? Is it something inherent to the game of baseball, or is it something within that class of human known as the fan? In other words, what's it all about?

Perhaps the best place to start is that curious phenomenon known as fandom. It seems that just about everyone is a fan of something or other, and it seems as if the objects of fandom become more numerous and diverse by the day. For instance, I was watching CNN coverage of the presidential primary election season in May of 2008 when I actually heard news anchor T. J. Holmes refer to candidate Barack Obama's "fanbase." Given its prodigious growth in today's world, one might assume that fandom is a rather recent feature of the human condition, borne of an advanced industrial order capable of producing cultural goods designed to elicit passive admiration from a mass audience willing to pay for the privilege. But rather than argue about the exact points of origin and the enabling conditions of fandom, it might be best at this point to examine how fans have been understood by those who care to examine fandom. How have fans been studied, and what conclusions have those studies drawn regarding the nature of fans?

While the formalized study of fandom is a rather recent development, the seeds of that study can be traced at least as far back as the 19th century, when the Industrial Age occasioned the birth of what can be generally referred to as "mass society." Preindustrial expressions of fandom notwithstanding, the many-to-one character of a mass societal focus on important, singular public entities embodies the way in which we often experience fandom in the current day—as members of a *crowd*; a mass audience that forges an adoring connection to something beyond its boundaries. This concept of the crowd figures prominently in the work of French psychologist Gustave Le Bon who, in 1895, published *The Crowd: A Study of the Popular Mind*. Writing in a time of class-based mass movements in the recently industrialized European societies, Le Bon was interested not only in the power of physical crowds to occupy and dominate a physical space, but also in the common mind that members of such crowds tended to share:

> Whoever be the individuals that compose it, however like or unlike be their mode of life, their occupations, their character, or their intelligence, the fact that they have been transformed into a crowd puts them in possession of a sort of collective mind which makes them feel, think, and act in a manner quite different from that in which each individual of them would feel, think, and act were he in a state of isolation.[1]

Are we at the ballpark yet? In describing what he termed the "psychological law of the mental unity of crowds,"[2] Le Bon rather accurately describes the conditions of fandom with which we've all become very familiar more than 100 years later. That being said, it's not necessarily a pretty picture. The notion of a thoughtful individual having his or her will erased and replaced by that of an unruly mob is not exactly flattering to the individual fan. But this is an almost complimentary view compared to some subsequent conceptions of fandom.

Historian Allen Guttmann points to the Neo-Marxist critique of spectator sports as one such conception. Compared to the earlier Marxist theory, which views sport spectators as a community of students taking lessons in proper citizenship, as embodied by the icons of athletic perfection on the playing field, the Neo-Marxists tend to view such activity as a debasement of the spontaneous play that occurs as a natural outgrowth of human existence. Why the about-face? Well, it probably has something to do with the influence of Sigmund Freud, who arrived on the scene just before some of those sport-loving Marxists morphed into Neo-Marxist party-poopers, and, as any sports fan will gladly tell you between innings and bites of his hot dog, that Freud dude is all about the sex, or, as Guttmann would phrase it:

> Neo-Marxist doctrine holds that capitalist society requires the repression and sublimation of sexual energy. The sexually repressed worker sublimates his erotic energies into productive labor, which brings in great profits for the capitalist owner. The psychological mechanisms of repression and sublimation are, however, imperfect. There is always the danger that the repressed energies cannot be totally sublimated in work. Unsublimated energies are potentially explosive and must be dealt with. Surplus repression which cannot be transformed into economic productivity benefiting the ruling class builds up frustration and threatens to upset the entire system of economic exploitation and political control.[3]

Before you know it, you're pouring a cup of warm beer on the foot of the out-of-towner sitting next to you and force-feeding him a giant foam finger! That's a main purpose of spectator sports in the Neo-Marxist worldview: to serve as a safety valve for the catharsis of all that pent-up frustration and repressed sexual energy that your boss couldn't milk out of you in the form of productive labor before you punched out on Friday. After all, if you don't get rid of it at the ballpark, it just might cause you to chop his head off on Monday morning, and that's certainly not good for the bottom line. Even if you're one of those cool, calm fans that would never lay a hand on even the most obnoxious opposing fan, this Neo-Marxist indictment of fandom has a category just for you. In fact, it's a place where most sports spectators reside in this view: on the couch next to a bag of chips. Rather than physically acting out, most fans settle for passive identification with the gladiators on the field, purging their surplus repression by proxy. The Neo-Marxists interpret this as a replication and reinforcement of the division of labor that is common in capitalist societies. The players play and the fans just watch, while all that anger and rage is directed toward the opposing team instead of the ruling class. Seriously, after screaming at the TV for nine innings, who's got the energy for a workers' revolution?

If we can get past the Neo-Marxist theoretical constructs and cumbersome jargon, this isn't too far removed from most current criticism of fans and their couch-potato lifestyles. Indeed, to the ear of a fan engrossed in an extra-inning game with the bases loaded and two out, there's not much difference between cries of "Workers of the world unite!" and "Put on some pants and go get a job already!" Both demands simply show no appreciation for the obvious pleasures of fandom. We know that there is economic injustice in this world, and that there is no substitute for hard work and ambition. But does that mean we have to turn off the ballgame? Well, fandom's critics seem to have come to terms with the notion that fans are not simply going to go away, as the last few decades have seen a less judgmental, more refined appreciation of the role of fandom in people's lives. Ironically, one source of this recent flourishing of fan studies can be found in the work of French sociologist Pierre Bourdieu, whose study of the process of cultural distinction is also informed by Marxist thought. Although trying to wade through Bourdieu's writing can feel like trying to find the exit of a maze while using the wrong map, his establishment of useful linkages to more recent approaches to the study of fandom makes it worth the effort.

Perhaps the initial cause of confusion regarding Bourdieu's work is the realization that this sociologist employs an *economic* framework in order to comprehend fandom. This merging of sociological concerns with those of economics is actually a staple of Marxist thought, and Bourdieu embraces this merger by examining the social reality of fandom as if it were an economic system. Beginning with the idea that different classes of people possess different types of capital in different concentrations, he proposes a system of social classes that exhibit different modes of fandom. Whether it's *cultural capital* derived from the schools one attended, *social capital* derived from one's network of personal acquaintances, or the *economic capital* found in one's bank account, these measures of value combine to determine how the members of each class make sense of their consumption of cultural products. This mix of the different capitals in which a social class invests constitutes what Bourdieu refers to as the *habitus* of that social class, which might be thought of as a set of conditions that are reflected in the attitudes and tastes of that class. Based on the attitudes and tastes that arise from this habitus, members of a particular social class become particular types of fans of particular types of things.

For example, most readers would probably acknowledge the existence of what might be termed an *upper class* at the pinnacle of society (what Bourdieu terms the *dominating fraction of the bourgeoisie*), the members of which are blessed with vast personal wealth (i.e., economic capital), a tight circle of powerful and connected friends (i.e., social capital), and fine educations from elite institutions (i.e., cultural capital). Most readers probably share an image of the tastes such people possess and how they display them: beautiful homes built by old money and acquired through inheritance, fully stocked wine cellars and the knowledge of viticulture required to consume them properly, and expensive collections of original works of art and the knowledge needed to interpret them properly. Put bluntly, these are not the people you'll find sitting next to you at the ballpark. In fact, Bourdieu claims that such folk would never deign to participate in any sort of fandom, for to do so would be perceived as undignified and beneath their station. Most readers are probably equally aware of a second social tier that exhibits some of the same annoying attitudes of exclusivity and elitism, but with a few noticeable differences. These folks might have attended the same elite schools as the upper class, but they did so for what they consider to be purer reasons that have little to do with fulfilling a familial legacy or reaping financial reward. In fact, pursuing material wealth and the traditionally valued objects it can buy is seen by these folks as a vulgar waste of time better spent on living a life of the mind. You might not find these people sitting next to you at the ballpark, either. But if you did, they'd somehow make you feel as if you were completely missing the point of what was happening on the field. Bourdieu labels this class the *dominated fraction of the bourgeoisie*, or what, in more familiar terms, might be viewed as bohemians or intellectuals. Though they might resist the characterization, these folks actually participate in fandom within Bourdieu's typology, but they do so in a rather specialized way:

> Intellectuals and artists have a special predilection for the most risky but also the most profitable strategies of distinction, those which consist in asserting the power, which is peculiarly theirs, to constitute insignificant objects as works of art or, more subtly, to give aesthetic redefinition to objects already defined as art, but in another mode, by other classes or class fractions (e.g., kitsch). In this case, it is the manner of consuming which creates the object of consumption, and a second-degree delight, which transforms the "vulgar" artifacts abandoned to common consumption, Westerns, strip cartoons, family snapshots, graffiti, into distinguished and distinctive works of culture.[4]

Perhaps we can add baseball to this list of "vulgar" entertainments that we all enjoy, but that are differently enjoyed, through a redefinition of it as a work of art by this social class of fans. In any case, it is clear that these folks feel they "get it" in a way that the average fan can't. Bourdieu suggests two additional classes that just don't get it: the *petit bourgeois*, the members of which know real culture when they see it, but feel more at ease confirming their possession of cultural capital by playing along at home while watching *Jeopardy* over dinner; and the *working class*, the members of which tend to cling to fandom as a pathetic substitute for the real cultural authority they lack.

But in all cases, other than the fan-deprived dominating fraction of the bourgeoisie, these classes of fandom might end up choosing the same cultural products to serve as their chosen objects of fandom. In other words, when attempting to comprehend what it means to be a fan, *what* fans consume might be less important than *how* they consume it. It's as if we're all at the same ballpark, but we're watching different ballgames. As easily accessed popular culture becomes the focus of cultural life, this sort of distinction between different fan cultures' consumption of the same fan objects tends to replace the traditional distinctions of "official" culture. This palate of new fan culture hierarchies became the focus of the next wave of fan culture studies.

A seminal figure in this next wave is John Fiske, whose scholarship is based on the premise that the pleasure fans derive from the consumption of popular culture exists as an opposing force to traditional bourgeois culture. For Fiske, being a fan is an essentially subversive activity, and the pleasure of fandom is actually a product of the modern fan's triumph over those old fossils who stood in front of the classroom, admonishing the captive students to turn off the television and read a book—one of the "right" books, chosen from that "Classics in the Cannon of Great Literature" handout that your dog ate while you were watching television. Freed from the restrictions imposed by those guardians of high culture standards, fans are able to choose from the panoply of popular culture texts that are widely available at the click of a button or the swipe of a credit card and that speak more directly to their own sensibilities. The pleasures of easy consumption and digestion ensue. Of course, there is an obvious dilemma in this tidy formula for fan empowerment: that cornucopia of popular entertainments from which the fan chooses her preferred weapon of cultural subversion is, on closer inspection, just a bunch of standardized, mass-produced industrial products marketed to the lowest common denominator of mass society in order to generate maximum profit for a bunch of greedy corporations. How subversive of the order could this possibly be? Enter the key to Fiske's conception of fandom: that notion of the *what* of consumption being less important than the *how*. For Fiske, many seemingly standardized popular culture products are what he terms *polysemic*—that is, they embody a variety of possible meanings, from which a fan can select those most relevant to his personal circumstances, and fashion them into a unique interpretation that sets him apart from other fans and the lumpen mass audience. Fan culture scholar Henry Jenkins mirrors this view in his claim that fandom revolves around "not exceptional texts, but rather exceptional readings."[5] Or, as Fiske himself would describe the battle, "Everyday life is constituted by the practices of popular culture, and is characterized by the creativity of the weak in using the resources provided by a disempowering system while refusing finally to submit to that power."[6] So, for Fiske, the market dominance of the few corporate producers of popular culture products can be effectively overcome by the millions of alternate readings conducted by the millions of fans in the consuming audience. This shift in focus from the mass marketing of standardized entertainment products to the level of individual fan activity is reflected in a parallel shift from the crowd psychology focus of Le Bon cited earlier to the psychological mechanisms developed and utilized by individual fans.

One possible explanation of fan behavior linked to individual psychology is suggested by the work of Melanie Klein, who examines child development in terms of what she identifies as the *paranoid-schizoid position* and *projective identification*. In her 1946 paper, "Notes on Some Schizoid Mechanisms," Klein describes the process by which an infant attempts to deal with good and bad feelings by internalizing the good ones as part of the self and expelling the bad ones. Once this paranoid-schizoid position of a split between "good self" and "bad self" feelings is established, the infant projects the latter onto the identity of the mother, thus preventing them from contaminating the former and facilitating the normal development of object relations.[7] In applying this model to adult fans rather than developing infants, the good-bad split of the paranoid-schizoid position remains intact, though the ensuing projective identification might not necessarily be limited to the bad. Because fans tend to view their fandom as an enjoyable and positive experience, perhaps it involves a projection of the fan's most positive hopes and desires onto the object of fandom. In this way, the fan sees his most cherished personal qualities as being shared by the object of his fandom. But what then becomes of the negative elements of this good-bad split? Since the paranoid-schizoid position is not necessarily resolved by this splitting, how might that bad part be used when one revisits it during times of anxiety and stress? Maybe those legions of Yankee haters could help answer that question, but this is an issue we will turn to later in this book.

More recent inquiries into fan psychology offer a specific application of this split between good and bad feelings to sports fans. Since any fan's team is destined to win some and lose some, sports fans are routinely faced with the need to deal not only with the elation of victory, but with the despair of defeat, as well. Projecting one's most positive personal attributes onto a team in the throes of a losing streak is a certain recipe for psychological confusion. At least one group of researchers contends that this contradiction is amplified by the strength of one's fandom, claiming that fans with a high degree of personal investment in a team not only exhibit healthier psychological profiles than less dedicated fans, but also experience more severe states of depression when their team loses.[8] In response to this dilemma, sports fans have developed various methods for coping with the threat of their team losing, as well as for using their team's victories to enhance psychological well-being.

When a fan's team is on a winning streak, one strategy used to positively associate that success with one's own psychological state is known as basking in reflected glory, or *BIRGing*. First suggested by Robert Cialdini and his team of researchers in a study of college football fans,[9] BIRGing is something that any fan of any sport should be able to recognize in her own behavior. Whenever fans drape themselves in officially licensed merchandise while reminiscing with fellow fans about how "we" kicked butt last Sunday, BIRGing is occurring. Whenever a clueless baseball fan in need of focus decides to follow the Yankees because history shows there's a good chance they'll win, he's involved in a type of preemptive BIRGing, which may have a prophylactic effect against any future psychological damage that would have resulted from rooting for a loser. Of course, some fans are a bit more risk-averse when it comes to linking their psychological health to their team's current success, especially if they know their team has a history of blowing it at the end of the season. Sociologist Daniel Wann and his associates[10] speak of a coping strategy just for them: *COFFing*, or cutting off future failure, through which a fan can preserve her positive psychological state by downplaying the current win streak of a team she fears will ultimately disappoint her. Additionally, Wann cites two related strategies for dealing with a team's failure that should be equally familiar to sports fans: cutting off reflected failure, or *CORFing*, which involves limiting one's identification with a losing team in order to preserve psychological well-being; and *blasting*, through which diehard fans incapable of CORFing due to their intense identification with their team simply trash the performance of the other team, the officials, the opposing fans, the guy selling snow cones, or just about anyone in order to feel better about rooting for a loser. For sports fans that may seem hopelessly antagonistic to one another's fortunes and psychological states, these four coping strategies may represent a rare point of harmony. Frankly, we've all been there before.

Yet another method for maintaining psychological health mentioned by Wann is *ingroup favoritism*, which involves fans' use of the biased perceptions of both fellow fans and rival fans.[11] This is the last refuge of the fan that has the misfortune of following a losing team, as the pain of defeat can be lessened by the belief that he's still a member of a superior group of fans. The importance of the entire fan community implied by this commonly used strategy highlights an important criticism applied to fan studies that focus on individual fan psychology or, as in Fiske's approach, the individual fan's ability to gain empowerment through individualized interpretations of mass culture fan texts. More recent study of the *executive fan* as an opinion leader and agenda setter for a fanbase has focused greater attention on the social hierarchies that develop within fandom.[12]

Matthew Hills has suggested that the central focus that Fiske gives to the degree of fan knowledge about the object of fandom (i.e., *fan cultural capital*) may be a reflection of the prominence of cultural capital in the prior formulations of Bourdieu, and he recommends that greater attention be devoted to a fan's status within a network of friends in the fanbase (i.e., *fan social capital*).[13]

It is this social realm of fandom that informs the method of this book, though it is my intent to mine that social realm while establishing virtually no access to physical groups of fans. Le Bon's notion of the *psychological crowd*, in which physical presence plays a less important role in group cohesion than thinking in unison, underlies the rationale for using the message boards found on Major League Baseball team Web sites as the site of data gathering for this study. These message boards constitute forums in which one can detect a rich hierarchy of fans, from the least knowledgeable casual observer to the deeply knowledgeable and obsessive executive fan. So, allow me to detail the method by which the fan narratives of Yankee hatred found in this book were gathered.

On June 10, 2008, the following message, titled *Who Hates the Yankees?*, was posted to the message boards on 29 of the 30 team Web sites of Major League Baseball:

> I'm not a (name of team) fan, but I have a question for those who are. It seems most baseball fans just don't like the Yankees. Some really hate them. It's almost like a family tradition for a lot of fans, dating back generations. If you consider yourself a Yankee hater, let me know why a (name of team) fan would feel that way. Is it lopsided trades? Free agents lured by Yankee dollars? Their fans? The pinstripes? Give me the details.

I should note that, for obvious reasons, I did not post the message to the New York Yankees' Web site and, for reasons unknown to me, the June 10 post to the Los Angeles Dodgers' Web site did not register and was reposted on June 12, 2008. Within 24 hours, I received a total of 154 responses to these postings, with an additional 17 responses arriving over the course of the next few days. Fans of every team were represented in this field of responses, ranging from 2 responses on the Seattle Mariners' Web site to a whopping 47 from fans posting to the Web site of the Pittsburgh Pirates. Unfortunately, my message and the responses it generated were deleted from the message boards on the Web sites of the Houston Astros, Milwaukee Brewers, and San Francisco Giants before I could download and save them. However, this deletion eliminated a total of only 12 responses, resulting in the retention of 93 percent of all fan responses. While I lament the lack of input from the fans of these three teams, I am confident that the remaining field of data represents the passion and diversity of opinion that baseball fans possess regarding this issue of Yankee hatred quite admirably.

Offered not so much as an inquiry in search of specific answers, my original message was structured as a sort of generalized probe intended to serve as an inducement for conversations among interested fans. Indeed, many of these fans eagerly engaged in spirited conversations; some rather sharply focused on hatred of the Yankees, while others wandered off on a variety of distantly related tangents. But the open-ended nature of this conversation is precisely what I sought to encourage, as it would allow for the fans themselves to control the course of the discussion without further interference from the person who had a motive for initiating it. Of course, this is a rather haphazard method of data collection. I eschewed the formalized control of the process a conventional interviewer might enjoy in order to preserve the spontaneity and honesty of fan expression that might otherwise have been lost. In fact, it was the desire to preserve this spontaneity and honesty that led me to reject the possibility of contacting a subset of these fans with follow-up questions designed to elicit more detailed opinions. I will freely admit that one reason for employing this method arises from the fact that I am not a trained social scientist skilled in the methods of survey research and interview technique. I'm sure that those who are trained in these methods would find much in my approach to object to, including the absence of a properly generated representative sample of baseball fans from which representative opinions could be gleaned. A common complaint arising from the lack of such a representative sample might be what some refer to as *self-selection bias*, a condition in which only those fans who are highly motivated and strongly opinionated select themselves as relevant and representative, merely by choosing to participate. Actually, I tend to view any such self-selection bias as a strength rather than a weakness. Pardon my lack of scientific rigor, but why shouldn't the most passionate and opinionated fans with the chutzpah to sit down at the keyboard and sound off receive the attention? At the very least, it seems that their contributions would result in a more entertaining read.

Actually, it's not just a lack of training or laziness on my part that resulted in a research method some might characterize as sitting back and collecting random reactions to my online "flaming." Significant evidence exists to support the efficacy of the online collection of ethnographic information that was once considered accessible only through interpersonal interaction. Jenkins notes that in engaging in practices like assembling and monitoring focus groups, rather than covertly observing pre-existing communities and their behaviors, ethnographic researchers have often been criticized for constructing the audience they seek to analyze.[14] Computer-mediated communication venues, such as Major League Baseball message boards, create an opportunity to observe a self-defined community that a researcher doesn't have to actively intervene in or contribute to. Even though my initial message to these message boards might constitute such an intervention or contribution, my avoidance of further participation allowed the discussion to take on a life of its own. In that way, the non-interventionist ethic of the participant-observer method so common to anthropological fieldwork is largely maintained. In addition to offering protection against the contamination threat posed by close contact with the researcher, online fan activity may also enhance a fan's willingness to contribute more openly to the dialogue created by a fanbase. Research reported by Adam Joinson reveals that self-disclosure is significantly higher when discussion participants interact through the use of computer-mediated communication rather than face-to-face meetings, largely due to the desirable feature of visual anonymity.[15] After all, if a fan and a fanbase cannot see one another, it becomes easier to assume that the members of the group share a particularly tight bond since the shared object of their fandom is the only point of discussion. Add to this the ability to participate in fan group activity during a time of one's own choosing, while wearing a bathrobe and messily masticating a bag of chips, and it becomes clear why fans might be a bit more willing to let it all hang out in an online environment. This effect is replicated in research on the computer-mediated disclosure of one's homosexuality, which indicates that online communication represents an opportunity for "disclosing a long-secret part of one's self."[16] Perhaps some baseball fans might see Web site message boards as a similar opportunity for disclosure of their long-secret, inner Yankee hater.

This enhanced opportunity for self-disclosure and the richer field of data that might result from it represents just one difference between online and offline fandom. Indeed, the very nature of the subjective fan experience might differ when fandom goes online. In his analysis of fans of the television program *X-Files*, Hills warns against assuming that the more passive, generalized fandom that tends to exist offline is simply replicated by online fandom in which participants are very aware "that other fans will act as a readership for speculations, observations and commentaries."[17] To be sure, the baseball fans that populate team website message boards are not only very aware of the increased intensity of fan interest that exists online, but also of the possibility that this very public forum for fan expression includes researchers that may be lurking about for the purpose of accumulating data. I encountered the following discussion among several fans of the Texas Rangers which exemplifies this heightened level of online suspicion regarding the reason for my query about Yankee hatred:

[Repsort writes] It's pretty sad that you have so much hatred in yourself that you have to post this on every board. Turn off the computer, go outside and get a life.[18]

[Xyzybaluba replies] And he waited twenty-four hours to be able to post! I mean, I hate the Yankees and all, but geesh![19]

[Mike E replies] Maybe he just had a surgery or something and it would be best to stay in. Or he's sick. Or he's doing a paper over it and this is the best way he knows how to get the most fans' opinions from various teams. Just throwing out ideas. I personally think he's here just to have more material to troll the Yankees with.[20]

[Purpledog replies] Me, I don't hate the players. I'm not real fond of the owners. And don't even get me started on their bandwagon fans. You must be one or you wouldn't be going around to all the boards asking such a stupid question.[21]

[Cpt.ranger replies] Whew, you guys are brutal. I'm diehard Rangers, but I wouldn't say get the hell out of my message boards. Most of these guys are just waiting for a juicy post to prey upon. As for me, I hate the Yankees but I have a scientific reason. I'm in the medical field so my hypothesis is that it is a male/female dominant trait passed on from generation to generation, and when two recessive partners (brainwashed Yankee heirs) mate, they create a genetically inferior and socially inept Yankees fan. Either that, or the kid watches so much ESPN that he is forced into rooting for the Yanks.[22]

Well, kudos to Mike E for arriving at the most accurate interpretation of my motives. But detective work aside, the overall tone of this discussion certainly reveals a level of passion that exceeds that of the casual offline fan.

Still, this sort of dedication to the fandom project should not be interpreted as license to accept fan *talk* as substantive fan *knowledge*. Hills cites the confusion of these two entities as a pernicious problem in some traditional ethnographic approaches to the study of fandom, noting a tendency to reduce fandom "to mental and discursive activity occurring without passion, without feeling, without an experience of (perhaps involuntary) self-transformation."[23] That fans seem to be quite knowledgeable regarding the objects of their fandom should not be taken as evidence that they are merely reservoirs of objective data. Asking why someone is a fan of something might yield less in the way of interpretive knowledge about the object of fandom than defensive, in-group justifications for being a fan. For this reason, the fan narratives about Yankee hatred found here must not be accepted as if they were truthful, whole cloth. Rather, I seek to interpret and analyze them in order to determine why this hatred is so important to these fans. In other words, my goal is not to present a field of objective information that would result in any rational reader's conversion to Yankee hatred. My goal is to assess why that hatred exists as an integral part of the subjective experience of so many baseball fans.

I believe this goal is best achieved by planting the seed of a discussion about Yankee hatred in the fertile soil of Major League Baseball team Web site message boards, letting it take root, and observing how it grows. Somehow, it seems as if directing a series of questions to select fans in a formal interview format would simply poison the well of fully formed opinion that already exists in these online fan communities. For that reason, I feel that this online collection of fan narratives of Yankee hatred represents an unusually pure and authentic field of data. But there is another reason for my decision to conduct this data gathering electronically: actually sitting down and talking face-to-face with these carbon-based life forms known as fans would create a needlessly large carbon footprint for this project. I can recall more than one puzzled look coming from my faculty colleagues when, in response to their assumptions that I'd be unavailable during the writing of this book due to extensive travel for interviewing and research, I told them they could just give me a call at home if they needed to speak with me. At the risk of constructing a Luddite self-image that appears to parallel that of the Unabomber, I made a decision several years ago to avoid unnecessary personal and professional travel in order to minimize my personal carbon footprint. While this has, at times, been difficult to achieve (I want my daughter to go to Disney World *without* me? No way!), I saw this project as an ideal opportunity for green professional development. So, in keeping with the earth-friendly spirit of this book, please avoid the temptation to read it while driving!

Finally, I'd like to offer something of a personal, full-disclosure statement. I am not, by any reasonable definition of the term, a baseball historian. But I have always been a baseball fan, and that fandom has outlived most of my other fan activities, be they focused on other sports, popular music, or movie stars. Perhaps this is because baseball provides an unusually rich and nuanced focus for fan activity; one that unfolds at a pace deliberate enough to allow for contemplation, reflection, and meaningful discussion among fans. Unlike the immediate pleasures offered by some other objects of fandom from my youth, these qualities seem to increase in importance as fans mature. So, this is primarily a book not about baseball, but about baseball fans. It is by no means a definitive work. It is just one attempt to make sense of something that I've always felt and that baseball fans of every allegiance seem to agree is out there.

So, Yankee hatred—what's it all about?

Chapter 2

IT'S ABOUT THE PLAYERS

While baseball fans tend to focus their attention on a particular team, the fact that those teams are comprised of individual players cannot be ignored. Fans are individual human beings, and individual players provide an opportunity for fans to form intimate, one-to-one relationships. Sure, these relationships are rooted in fantasy. But what aspect of fandom isn't, and what fan fantasizes about what it would be like to actually be an entire team? A kid dreams of emulating the on-field performance of his favorite player, not the general style of play that characterizes his team of choice. After all, a team's style of play is largely determined by a team's manager, who attempts to get the most out of the roster given to him. Perhaps some kids dream of manipulating on-field talent (a dream that seems to find increasingly frequent expression as baseball simulation games and fantasy leagues proliferate), but I would think that more of them dream of actually playing the game. It's the difference between being the hero who wins it with a walk-off homer and the middle management bureaucrat who sits in the dugout worrying and wondering if others can get the job done. Kids play. Players play. And when kids grow up to be adult fans of the game, it is the player on the field that reminds them of what that used to be like.

So, when a player leaves your team—a player around whom you've constructed one of those intimate, one-to-one relationships, fueled by fantasy and remembrance of a youth when any heroic exploit was still possible—you take it personally. If that player happens to leave your team for the Yankees, the sting of that loss is amplified in ways that this book can only begin to articulate. Of course, players leave teams for any number of reasons and under a variety of circumstances, and who better than the scorned fan to articulate the acute pain of losing a favorite player—for any reason, under any circumstances—to the New York Yankees.

Let's begin with the phenomenon of the *stolen player*—a fan favorite snatched away by one of the many temptations dangled by the most storied franchise in Major League Baseball. The implication here is that, had the Yankees not used their superior bargaining position to acquire him, the player in question would certainly have led your team to a string of World Series victories within your lifetime (remember, it's all about the fantasy, right?). As it happens, the most extensive fan discussion regarding the stolen player phenomenon is provided by fans of a team with a relatively recent history of World Series victories—the Oakland Athletics (A's), winners of the Fall Classic in 1972, 1973, 1974, and 1989. Many of the A's fans who are currently in a position to gripe about the Yankees stealing their players were actually alive to witness these triumphs in person. But just think how many more championships would have been celebrated in Oakland had the Yankees kept their greedy hands in their pinstriped pockets. Oh, what might have been!

This discussion among A's fans begins with three stolen players from those championship teams of the 1970s, who would end up wearing Yankee pinstripes: Jim "Catfish" Hunter, Ken Holtzman, and Reggie Jackson. Holtzman, a starting pitcher, and Jackson, an outfielder, arrived in New York after first being traded to the Baltimore Orioles on April 2, 1976, in a deal that brought outfielder Don Baylor, and pitchers Mike Torrez and Paul Mitchell to Oakland. Holtzman would soon arrive in New York through a multiplayer trade on June 15, 1976, accompanied by catcher Ellie Hendricks and pitchers Doyle Alexander, Jimmy Freeman, and Grant Jackson, for catcher Rick Dempsey and pitchers Tippy Martinez, Rudy May, Scott McGregor, and Dave Pagan.[1] Jackson, an eventual Hall of Famer, was granted free agency at the end of the 1976 season and signed a contract with the Yankees on November 29, 1976.[2] Future Hall of Fame pitcher Jim "Catfish" Hunter went directly from the A's to the Yankees, signing a free agent contract on December 31, 1974.[3] Although the indirect routes to New York taken by Holtzman and Jackson are not mentioned by the discussants, this only serves to reinforce the focus on the Yankees as the beneficiaries of the "theft." Let's join the discussion as Sweegger and Salbando6 debate the claim that there are two types of Northern California baseball fans who choose to follow the Yankees:

> [Sweegger writes] I can see if you're from NY you will probably love the Yanks and more power to you. But you grow up in Northern California and become a Yanks fan? There's only two types of people who do that: 1) the

guys that like the baby-blue Yankee hat; 2) Band wagon jumpers who didn't have enough sense to become Red Sox fans when the ship started to sink in the Bronx.[4]

[Salbando6 replies] Actually Sweegger, you forgot #3: Those that were around when Catfish, Holtzman and then Reggie went to the Yankees and gave up on [former A's owner and General Manager Charlie] Finley's team in 1977 when he sold/traded everyone. Oddly enough, the championships that Cat & Reggie brought to Oakland moved to NY with them. Things were so bad in A's land that by 1978, I went to Giants games just to see Vida [Blue, former A's pitcher]. And the Yanks had Reggie, Catfish, [former A's pitcher Paul] Lindblad and Holtzman. To a twelve-year-old (me), they were the "A's in Pinstripes." Charlie may have given up on them, but I didn't. And it's not baby blue, it's navy. The Denver Nuggets are baby blue. Also, as far as buying this or that (including [pitcher Roger] Clemens), my opinion is that method of operation is over for the Yanks, now that George [Steinbrenner, Yankees owner] has turned over the control of the club to his sons. The "New" Yankees (buying the biggest free agents) is a four-way tie between the Dodgers, Angels, Mets & Red Sox.[5]

[Sweegger replies] #3 might be covered under #2 with an extension to disillusioned fans, not just bandwagon jumpers. I'll leave that up to you because those events happened a generation b4 me and I didn't have to experience it. After all, I'm somewhat of a [St. Louis] Cards "fan" after seeing Tony [LaRussa, former A's manager] and Mark [McGwire, former A's player] go over to the NL and I still think Tony's the best manager ever (and I just loved seeing them deflate the Tigers). But then again, if the A's play the Cards I root for the A's all the way.[6]

[Salbando6 replies] Baby blue and pink? Yep, I've seen 'em. A's have them, too. I'm really just fond of the normal 50/50 hats. All the variations don't do it for me though. Basically, if the players don't wear it, it's not for me . . . so I'm definitely with you on that. Yep, I was an A's die hard. But (like the 70s) it tore me up to see them dismantle the team in the 90s after [Jose] Canseco and McGwire put Oakland back on the map. A lot of that was due to [former A's General Manager] Sandy Alderson & Co betting heavily on the Giants departure (and losing big-time). There are ramifications that still exist today because of that blunder. But the way they handled the Canseco trade, dumped Stew [former A's pitcher Dave Stewart], and Walter [Weiss, former A's shortstop] made me see them differently. Now, of course, revamping the team happens all the time with Billy [Beane, A's General Manager], but from '87–'92, it felt like it would last forever . . . So, today, I admire them for what they accomplish, but EXPECT them to go elsewhere. I am amused at the "traitor" cheers when [former A's first baseman Jason] Giambi comes to the plate, but other than Chavvy [A's third baseman Eric Chavez], who stays very long? Even Swish [former A's outfielder Nick Swisher] signed a nice long contract . . . to still end up traded. I can't deal with that.[7]

From Sweegger's rather general complaint about Oakland-area "band-wagon jumpers" and fans with a non-regulation fashion sense regard-ing headgear, a detailed recollection of stolen players and stolen glory emerges. Significantly, it does so as a corrective, as Salbando6 proposes a third category of Northern California Yankee fan generated by an allegiance to stolen players that is greater than the allegiance to the team from which they were stolen. Of course, the players mentioned were not literally stolen by the Yankees, and Salbando6 acknowledges this fact. Still, his reaction to the situation was that of someone victimized by an illegitimate loss—attending San Francisco Giants games across the Bay as if exercising visitation rights to a former A's player, and following the "A's in Pinstripes" as they won championships that could have stayed local. Salbando6 is certainly aware that being 12-years-old accounts for his allegiance to these players being greater than that of A's management, yet his resentment of the A's owner for giving up on them is still palpable. He readily admits that his own childhood experience with Yankee thiev-ery might not apply today, as he goes on to cite several teams that now qualify as the "New Yankees" in this regard.

Torn between supporting his team and remaining loyal to his stolen on-field heroes performing in exile, Salbando6 seems to embody what Hills terms "multiple fandoms."[8] For most fans, the focus of fandom is often not a single object, but a variety of objects, either related or distinct, enabling various aspects of self-identity to be expressed at different times in the fan's life. Perhaps the need for one-to-one identification with par-ticular players was simply more important to Salbando6 at age 12 than an absolute allegiance to his home team. Indeed, the focus of his fandom in adult life seems to have shifted away from stolen players to whom he would have felt an obligation of loyalty in his youth toward a less strident, almost melancholy adherence to his team. Citing a second purge of star players during his adulthood, he now seems resigned to the fact that his team will be periodically dismantled and rebuilt; he admires the players on his team, but expects them to eventually be stolen away. Sweegger exhibits a similar shift in his objects of fandom over time, claiming to now be something of a Cardinals fan based upon the migration of a favorite manager and star player from Oakland to St. Louis. Still, he hedges his bets, reserving the right to remain an A's fan if and when they play the Cardinals.

In his comparison of fans and their objects of fandom to Narcissus gaz-ing upon his watery reflection, Cornel Sandvoss emphasizes that, in both cases, we're dealing with a fragile dynamic.[9] Just as the wind or a pebble might cause the water to ripple, thus distorting Narcissus' reflection, so can the object of one's fandom be altered by a player's exodus, changing one's relationship to the team or player as objects of fandom. That said,

Sandvoss notes that fans are prepared to adjust to such changes in order to preserve the investment made in linking self-identity with the object of fandom.[10] Fans don't control the object of their fandom, and it does not control them. Rather, they exist in a reciprocal relationship in which accommodating change becomes a necessity. Both Sweegger and Salbando6 seem to reflect this imperative, each having morphed into a different type of fan as the object of their fandom morphed into something it once was not. That favorite players have been stolen away is secondary to the need to preserve the extension of self that their fandom represents. So, the sting of loss felt when childhood heroes become Yankees evolves into an adult acceptance of the inevitable as a means of preserving fan identity in an unstable environment. But if allegiance to the team eventually trumps allegiance to stolen players who are no longer with the team, what becomes of those stolen players? Does the fan simply define them as neutral entities, directing any animosity over their loss toward the thieving team, or do such players become the enemy? More specifically, will fans reject their favorite players if and when they become Yankees?

Pliny the Younger, who long ago offered this critique of fans of chariot racing in ancient Rome, hints at an answer to this question:

> I can find nothing new or different in [the races]: once seen is enough, so it surprises me all the more that so many thousands of adult men should have such a childish passion for watching galloping horses and drivers standing in chariots, over and over again. If they were attracted by the speed of the horses or the drivers' skill, one could account for it, but in fact it is the racing colors they really support and care about, and if the colors were to be exchanged in mid-course during a race, they would transfer their favor and enthusiasm and rapidly desert the famous drivers and horses whose names they shout as they recognize them from afar. Such is the popularity and importance of a worthless shirt.[11]

I doubt that any of the worthless shirts Pliny refers to bore pinstripes. Still, baseball fans often cite examples of players they once admired becoming somehow changed for the worse simply by virtue of donning a Yankee uniform. As Arizona Diamondbacks fan No1baxfan observes, "Something cruel and unusual happens to a player when they become a Yankee."[12]

Of course, the Yankees' sizeable revenue stream is frequently cited as a corrupting influence on players once viewed as likeable—prior to their move to New York. Natsfan11, a Washington Nationals fan, mentions outfielder Johnny Damon as a prime example of this phenomenon, claiming to have "loved him with the Red Sox, but he seemed like he was lured by money to the Yankees."[13] Indeed, Damon's income rose from $8.25 million in 2005 to $13 million upon signing as a free agent with the Yankees in

2006.[14] A similar complaint of how Yankee dollars precede the pinstripes as a source of negative player transformations comes from Chgophil, a Chicago White Sox fan, who recalls that in 2003, relief pitcher Tom Gordon "had a nice comeback season with the White Sox, but said in negotiations that he only wanted to go to a team that would make him the closer. Then where does he go? To the team with future Hall of Fame closer Mariano Rivera."[15] Once again, it appears that a fan's suspicion is justified, as Gordon would earn a save in only 4 of the 15 games he finished in relief with the Yankees in 2004, as opposed to the 12 saves in 35 games he finished in relief with the White Sox during the previous year.[16]

While money might be the most obvious factor to which change in a player is attributed after a move to New York, some fans detect a more subtle influence in the organizational culture of the Yankees. Kansas City Royals fan Blu4evr locates this source of ruin directly inside the Yankees' clubhouse:

> I also hate what they do to players. They make them shave, cut their hair, dress up, and dance whenever a Steinbrenner plays a fiddle. I guess I'm more of a fan of clubhouses like the A's, which is basically an adult frat house, except with slightly less beer.[17]

While restrictions on players' personal grooming seem to have lessened since control of the Yankees' daily operations passed from George Steinbrenner to his son, Hank, this reputation of the Yankees' clubhouse as a site of intolerance for individual expression has been a focus for Yankee hatred throughout the Steinbrenner era. In any case, when trying to identify a reason why once-loved players change for the worse when they become Yankees, the influence of Yankee dollars and the demands of conformity that come with it seem to be worth more than those worthless shirts.

It's rather easy for most of us to appreciate how the tangible effects of money and arbitrary dress codes can generate resentment of the Yankees among many baseball fans—the former is something that is in relatively short supply among many fans and their teams, while the latter chafes against the cherished American value of individual freedom. But sometimes Yankee hatred comes from a far less rational place. Sometimes it is expressed, without any objective reasoning to support it, as blind hatred of certain players on a purely personal level. This seems to have little to do with perceived material greed, capitulation to authoritarian owners, on-field performance, or any other measureable quality. It has to do with hatred at a primal level; a visceral, negative reaction to a player's essence as a human being. Of course, these human beings just happen to be wearing pinstripes.

I find it an encouraging sign that this sort of ad hominem attack was offered up rather infrequently by fans. Still, briefly mentioning just a few might provide a peek into a reservoir of primitive impulses that most fans manage to quell even during spirited discussions. Pittsburgh Pirates fan Mattmel17, in his cogent critique of Yankee third baseman Alex Rodriguez, proclaims, "A-Rod drinks Zima!!"[18] Datsyuk13, a Detroit Tigers fan, pulls no punches in announcing, "I hate Derek Stupid Jeter! He's got a face only a fist could love."[19] Travelingmsfan1 plays the role of voodoo priest on the White Sox message boards when he offers the following: "I think Giambi and A-Rod have a curse on them, and as long as those two are on the roster, they won't win another World Series."[20]

Not all of the Yankee hatred directed at individual players has such mystical, interior origins. Specific incidents of actual on-field play have sometimes resulted in animosity dating back generations. One might think that the passage of time would blur the details of play on the field, and that current Yankee hatred could simply be attributed to a reservoir of vague, negative feelings. Chgophil's recollection of his own Yankee hatred, starting "in the late 1970s with the arrogance of Reggie Jackson," typifies this generalized origin of the phenomenon, which is based in a perceived attitude or character trait.[21] Some can actually pinpoint the precise moment their Yankee hatred began. Atlanta Braves fan Chopinchip is one such fan, describing his moment of conversion as follows:

> I hate the Yankees for one simple reason—Jim "I love 'roids like candy" Leyritz bombing a hanging slider off of Mark Wohlers in the '96 World Series. That had to be one of the most crushing experiences of my life.[22]

Unsupported suggestions of substance abuse notwithstanding, Chopinchip accurately recalls that moment in the eighth inning of Game Four of the 1996 World Series when Leyritz hit a three-run homer, a moment often cited as the turning point in a series eventually won by the Yankees. Toronto Blue Jays fan Jaysfan feels the need to resort to self-censored profanity in order to recall the origin of his Yankee hatred, claiming that "ever since that piece of sh*t Bucky Dent hit the home run in 1978 when I was a [Red] Sox fan, I have hated the Yankees. [In] 1979, I started following the Jays."[23] Jaysfan is certainly not the only baseball fan to remember this moment from a one-game playoff against the Red Sox for the American League East title, which propelled the Yankees toward a World Series victory. However, the fact that a single moment could not only create a Yankee hater, but also cause that Yankee hater to abandon his team of choice, might explain the need for an expletive.

These two examples of on-field plays resulting in Yankee hatred seem to represent a simple calculus: the heroics of a Yankee dash the championship hopes of the opposing team, and Yankee hatred ensues. But one fan offers a pair of reasons that transcend the loss of a mere game. In describing the origin of his own Yankee hatred, Cleveland Indians fan JoeyEuclid simply states, "Yankee players f@#cked up the careers of Ray Chapman and Herb Score."[24] The case of Chapman is certainly the more severe of the two, and describing it as merely the destruction of a career is certainly an understatement. On August 16, 1920, a fifth-inning plate appearance by the Indians' shortstop in a game against the Yankees ended in what, to this day, is the only death caused by a pitched ball in the history of Major League Baseball. Struck in the left temple by a fastball thrown by submarine-style pitcher Carl Mays, Chapman actually walked off the field with the assistance of two teammates.[25] But he would lose consciousness after arriving at New York's St. Lawrence Hospital, dying the following morning after unsuccessful brain surgery.[26] While the Indians quickly recovered from this tragedy, replacing Chapman with Joe Sewell and finishing the season by winning their first World Series, it appears that some fans still bear a grudge. Perhaps it is the finality of the Chapman incident that accounts for its identification as a cause of Yankee hatred almost 90 years later.

The second player mentioned by JoeyEuclid as a source of Yankee hatred may have met a less catastrophic fate on the field of play, but the case of Herb Score represents a fresher wound for many Indians fans. Making his debut in 1955, Score appeared to be the next standout pitcher in an already exceptional starting rotation that featured three future Hall of Famers in Bob Feller, Bob Lemon, and Early Wynn. Score led the American League in strikeouts that year, being named an All-Star and Rookie of the Year. His sophomore season was even more impressive, as he repeated his performance as League strikeout leader and All-Star while winning 20 games.[27] Off to another fine start in the 1957 season, Score took the mound against the Yankees on May 7. In the first inning, infielder Gil McDougald hit a scorching line drive that struck Score in the right eye. Though Score recovered from the injury, his prospects for joining Feller, Lemon, and Wynn in the Hall of Fame quickly faded upon his return to the mound in 1958. He would pitch for only 5 more seasons, retiring in 1962 before reaching the age of 30. Fans could only speculate as to the precise cause of Score's declining performance. One possibility is related to a change Score made in his pitching motion to better shield himself from batted balls, which some say resulted in a decline in the velocity of his blazing fastball.[28] Others cite an arm injury incurred after his return to pitching in 1958 as the problem.[29] There are reports of Score himself saying that he was already developing a sore arm at the time of the McDougald incident.[30] But whatever the cause of the decline in his abilities, fans endured the pain of witnessing that decline on the field. Unlike the Chapman case, in which fans experienced the complete denial of a player's future, they were surely preoccupied with thoughts of what might have been each time Score took the mound as a shadow of his former self. For this reason—along with an enduring fondness borne of his later career as a broadcaster for the Indians—the ruin of Herb Score's playing career by the random path of a batted ball remains a potent source of Yankee hatred for Indians fans.

That the unintended consequence of a single plate appearance continues to generate Yankee hatred many decades after the fact might seem a bit harsh. Yet, some fans seem to harbor a genuine affection for certain players in pinstripes, despite an avowed distaste for the team. Former Yankee first baseman Don Mattingly often appears on that list, perhaps due to the fact that the Yankees failed to win a single championship while he was in uniform. Paul O'Neill joins Mattingly as a player who can occasionally transcend Yankee hatred, despite his role as a contributor to the Yankee hegemony of the late 1990s. But the Yankee for whom fans most frequently express fondness—a fondness that often borders on sympathy—is Mickey Mantle.

As the career of Mickey Mantle has been more exhaustively examined than perhaps that of any player in the last 50 years, recounting the specifics here would be an exercise in redundancy for many readers. Suffice it to say that Mantle's career was characterized by magnificent achievement in the face of constant physical ailments—some attributable to sports-related injuries dating back to his teenage years, and others attributable to a less-than-healthy lifestyle. Indeed, fascination with Mantle's career might, to some extent, be fueled by the same "what might have been" mentality that the careers of Chapman and Score foster in the minds of fans. That said, there is scant evidence that such feelings regarding Chapman and Score extend beyond the home-team fanbase. Mantle seems to invoke a nostalgia that transcends current team allegiances, recalling an era just prior to the one that fans readily admit has cultivated a certain cynicism about the game in general and the Yankees in particular. Arizona Diamondbacks fan Grammoxox offers a concise distillation of this phenomenon:

Loved the 1956 WS [World Series]. Loved that team and Mantle was my hero. After that, I just didn't care. The Dodgers moved to LA, where I lived and there was [pitcher Sandy] Koufax and [pitcher Don] Drysdale. Then Steinbrenner bought the team and my active hate began. Arrogant, elitist, obnoxious jerk! I really think between dear George and Yankee fans, Yankee players turn into arrogant, elitist, obnoxious jerks!"[31]

Boston Red Sox fan Theroostah expands upon this analysis in a response to a Yankee fan's comment:

> Over the years, the Yanks have had some very good and decent ballplay-ers, such as Bernie Williams, or Jeter, or Paul O'Neill, but the Yankee front office and their fans' boorishness only lowered those ballplayers' stature. Mickey Mantle is an excellent example of that. He was a dumb country hick with tremendous talent, but the Yankee PR guys set him up to be the "next coming" and almost destroyed him psychologically. Read your team's history and you'll discover they had to send The Mick back down to the minors and change his number from [Babe Ruth's number] six to seven just to relieve the pressure that was placed on his young and naïve shoulders.[32]

That a Red Sox fan might offer such a sympathetic defense of a Yankee player is stunning, indeed. Yet, it is significant that both Theroostah and Grammoxox ground their supportive statements about Mantle in a critique of the Yankees organization.

It is not just nostalgia for Mantle and other players about what is per-ceived to be an era of innocence and purity that accounts for these defenders of Yankees within other teams' fanbases. An additional factor in the equation seems to involve the process through which some players become Yankees. New York Mets fan 3bwright articulates a distinction that many fans view as a vital criterion for judging whether a Yankee player is worthy of praise or hatred:

> Some players that they drafted and brought up through their system are okay. Players that went for the money—hate them.[33]

The issue 3bwright raises refers to a major dividing line among fans regarding their feelings toward individual players: the homegrown player versus the free agent. The generally positive view of players like Mantle may have less to do with nostalgia for the individual player than with nos-talgia for the business model under which baseball operated prior to the era of free agency. After the abolition of Major League Baseball's reserve clause in 1970, the game's balance of power clearly swung in the direc-tion of the players, as the concept of the free agent replaced the notion that a team might lay claim to the services of a player throughout his entire career. As a result, the idea that the good player is a *team* player was brought into question as players assumed a sort of independent contractor status. But as any baseball fan can tell you, there's no "I" in "team." So, how can a fan love a player who values his freedom to bargain a contract more than his dedication to the team and the community it represents?

As a player whose career predates the advent of free agency, Mickey Mantle certainly avoids this dilemma by providing fans an iconic example of the homegrown player who spent the entirety of his career in a single team's uniform. That his uniform featured Yankee pinstripes seems to make little difference to the many fans that admire him. Even Yankees of the current free agent era sometimes enjoy this exemption from hatred if the fans perceive them as homegrown, with Derek Jeter being a frequently mentioned player in this category. Conversely, players who become Yankees through free agency enjoy this hatred exemption much less frequently, especially if they are considered by fans to be of superstar status. Indeed, the phenomenal salaries commanded by free agent superstars strongly reinforce the sense that such players are motivated by money rather than a dedication to the team. The following conversation between Cincinnati Reds fan TS20 and HolyCanoli, a Yankee fan visiting the Reds message boards, indicates that negative feelings about the Yankees' willingness to spend lavishly on free agent superstars is not limited to fans of those other 29 teams:

[TS20 writes] One reason the Yanks have tanked since the wild spending is that wild spending doesn't bring a team together. Teams have to have a cohesiveness and too many big fish rot the pond. Bringing in one superstar after another doesn't get the ring. Sure, it will most likely get you to the postseason, but to be a champion, a team has to play together and play as a team, sacrificing at times. In a short series, everything is magnified, and little things have cost the Yankees in recent years. They also haven't developed a very good farm system. So, as [pitcher Mike] Mussina and [pitcher Andy] Pettitte go their ways, they will purchase new pitchers and hope for the best. I said I love Yankee history before Stein[brenner], but not since the out of control spending.[34]

[HolyCanoli replies] I totally agree with you in the sense that bringing in superstar after superstar will not win you anything. When you look at the Yankee teams that won in the late 90s, they played as a team. They fought for each other and really showed a passion that isn't there anymore. Now, they've all made their big pay day and there's no more fire. Fortunately for us Yankee fans, they are moving to an approach that builds from within. They could have easily traded [homegrown pitcher Phil] Hughes and [homegrown pitcher Ian] Kennedy and [homegrown second baseman Robinson] Cano and [homegrown outfielder Melky] Cabrera for [pitcher Johan] Santana or others but they chose to stick with the young talent. Hopefully, in time, this will bring on new success.[35]

Even though he arrived in New York via trade rather than free agency, Alex Rodriguez seems to personify the negative opinion fans hold about the high-priced free agent superstar. After all, it is widely believed that the

Yankees were perhaps the only team capable of assuming the gargantuan salary Rodriguez had secured through his 2001 free agent contract with the Texas Rangers once the Rangers decided that the financial burden could no longer be tolerated. So, the stigma of being a free agent superstar stuck with Rodriguez as he began his career as a Yankee in 2004. Still, for those rare fans able to muster a kind word for Rodriguez, their sympathies are often rooted in his perceived mistreatment by a Yankees organization that seems to think its copious wealth should determine how the game is played between the lines. Kansas City Royals fan Bfos embodies this sentiment in criticizing the Yankees' decision to recast Rodriguez as a third baseman in order to make room for him in their star-studded lineup:

> I've always liked A-Rod. He should have stayed at SS [shortstop]. He really gave up a lot in that move because he was a much better SS than Jeter.[36]

This brief comment articulates a rather common theme expressed by fans regarding the relationship between the high-priced superstars of the free-agent era and the team perceived as their prime destination: when the Yankees choose to embrace the high-priced superstar, the organization will share with the player any fan resentment that may ensue. Perhaps that special relationship between the individual fan and the individual player, formed in the fantasies of childhood and cited at the beginning of the chapter, accounts for this theme. Indeed, if our icons of athleticism can be somewhat preserved by having the guys in the front office shoulder some of the blame for sullying our fantasies with money, then so be it!

Of course, childhood fans grow into an adulthood in which fandom becomes a bit more rational and measured as fantasies of on-field glory are erased by age. Simply shifting the blame from wealthy player to wealthy organization begins to seem a little simplistic. The ambivalence of the mature fan regarding these dual targets for resentment is nicely expressed by another Kansas City Royals fan, Blu4evr:

> I'll admit it. I'm a Yankees hater. It's a combination of a lot of things. I'm too young to remember the rivalries of the 70s, but I can remember the doldrums of the late 90s, when it seemed as though they were ruining the game by buying every premium free agent on the market. Frustration turned to rage, I guess . . . Props to them for trying to be competitive, and I'm normally a staunch free-market defender, but baseball is no place for cutthroat economics. It should be a place for cutthroat baseball.[37]

An even greater easement for the Yankees' willingness to use their wealth to enhance their prospects for winning comes from Pittsburgh Pirates fan, Srs5020:

I can honestly say that I used to be one of the many baseball fans who hated the Yankees with a passion primarily because they went out and bought big name free agents year in and year out. But, they are playing by the rules. Nothing in baseball says that they can't go out and buy whoever they want every year.[38]

As I read Srs5020's words, I can't help but detect an unexpressed, long-repressed wish that those rules by which the Yankees are playing should be different; that *something* in baseball should say that they can't just go out and buy whoever they want every year. It's difficult to lay all of one's hatred on the Yankees when they are simply doing what Major League Baseball allows them to do. Yes, players can be greedy. But if fans reject the players, what is left to be a fan of? In fairness to the players, it should be noted that at least one incident in the Yankees' history as the dominant franchise in Major League Baseball stands as a reminder to fans that their beloved players may, at times, join them in the role of helpless victim. In 1954, well before the era of multimillion-dollar player contracts, American League owners approved the sale of the Philadelphia Athletics to Chicago businessman Arnold Johnson, who planned to move the team to Kansas City, despite several bids by other potential owners, which would have kept the Athletics in Philadelphia. Not only was this a blow to the fans of Philadelphia, it was a move that would enhance the prospects of the Yankees for many years to come. Johnson, one-time owner of Yankee Stadium and a long-standing business associate of Yankees owners Dan Topping and Del Webb, may have been responsible for introducing Major League Baseball to Kansas City, but few thought his intention was to bring the fans in that city a winner. It soon became apparent that if any promising young player showed up on the Kansas City roster, he would quickly be traded to the Yankees for some combination of over-the-hill players and cash. Perhaps the most notable player to come through this Kansas City pipeline was a young Roger Maris, who would quickly become a home-run record breaker with the Yankees. But even more jaw-dropping is the case of Yankee pitcher Ralph Terry who, in 1957, was traded to Kansas City for a package of eight nondescript players. At the time of the trade, Terry was an unrefined talent badly in need of seasoning at the Major League level, which the Yankees could not provide without risking their string of championships. After getting that seasoning for two years in a Kansas City uniform, the new and improved Ralph Terry was traded back to the Yankees for Jerry Lumpe and a couple of mediocre pitchers, where he became a 20-game winner.[39] This obvious conflict of interest between Johnson and the Yankees almost certainly extended New York's championship streak during the 1950s and 1960s. Yet, the Yankees were merely doing what Major League Baseball allowed them to do. While Maris, Terry, and many other players would be targeted by Yankee haters as they earned their World Series rings, far more players would languish along with the fans of Kansas City, helpless pawns in a game where everyone was just following the rules.

Clearly, saddling players with blame for the negative influence arising from the money they are paid places the fans' most intimate linkage to the game in serious jeopardy. After all, those wealthy players are only the recipients of that bounty; they don't directly wield it as an instrument of power capable of determining which teams win and which teams lose, or which fans cheer and which fans cry. What fans seem to agree on is the notion that buying a championship is an act worthy of hatred, whether that act is attributed to the Yankees management, in particular, or the structure of Major League Baseball in general. It is this pair of forces, which play outside the lines, to which the next chapter will turn.

Chapter 3

IT'S ABOUT THE SYSTEM

Originally, my intentions for addressing the Yankees organization and Major League Baseball as inducements for Yankee hatred involved the writing of two separate chapters. But as I studied the comments of fans focused on these two topics, it became apparent that separating them would represent something of a false distinction. For some fans, complaints about one of these entities necessarily invoke the other as an accomplice, as if collusion and conspiracy were unavoidable characteristics of their relationship to one another. For others, that relationship is seen as less symbiotic than compensatory, where an inability on the part of Major League Baseball to exert authority creates a vacuum that the Yankees organization aggressively fills to its own advantage. In either case, it is clear that baseball fans perceive the Yankees and Major League Baseball as inseparable parts of a system; a two-headed monster which, according to the final balance sheet, produces various strains of enmity within the fanbases of those other 29 teams.

So, let's begin with the more direct focus for hatred of this system: the Yankees organization. As the half of this system that is immediately identifiable with the on-field product of Yankees baseball, it is this organization—the general manager, the front office, the ownership—that tends to be the initial target for negative fan comments. And those comments are often just as generalized as the average fan's understanding of that organization's internal workings. Perhaps the term most commonly used to characterize those workings is *evil*. Transpose this term onto the Yankees' perceived position as the reigning imperial power of Major League Baseball, and the following comment from the message boards of the Washington Nationals seems rather inevitable:

> Every right-thinking human being hates the Yankees. As my son often says when trading barbs with opposing fans leaving [Baltimore's] Camden Yards, "Well, at least we can all agree that we hate the Yankees." Why? Why did Luke hate the empire?[1]

This *Star Wars*-inspired reference to what Boston Red Sox co-owner Larry Lucchino dubbed "the evil empire" is echoed in this exchange between two Atlanta Braves fans:

> [2run homer writes] I like the Yankees. I don't like the aura of the evil empire, though.[2]
> [Abrave1 replies] You can't have one without the other. That's who they are. George [Steinbrenner] = Darth Vader.[3]

A similar sentiment is expressed by Cowhide, a Kansas City Royals fan, although his comment abandons any reference to the world of entertainment and invokes one from the world of everyday reality, embodying more of a resignation to the inevitable than light humor:

> Oh, back in the day, we had one heck of a rivalry and never could quite get to the World Series because of the Yankees. And this was exacerbated by ABC-TV, in particular, openly pulling for the Yankees during the playoffs. But that all ended for me when [Royals' third baseman] George Brett went deep on [Yankees' pitcher] Goose Gossage way back in 1980. And the pine tar home run three years later was just icing on the cake. I don't hate the Yankees anymore. That's like hating IBM.[4]

Although I'm guessing that the first home run to which Cowhide refers is Brett's game-winning shot in the third and final game of the 1980 American League Championship Series, the "pine tar home run" is an incident that is burned into the consciousness of fans with far less detailed memories than Cowhide possesses. Now recognized as a major piece of recent baseball lore, the incident involves yet another meeting of Brett and Gossage at Yankee Stadium in which Brett hit a ninth-inning homer to put the Royals in the lead. After Brett rounded the bases and returned to the Royals' dugout, Yankees' manager Billy Martin complained that Brett's bat was smeared with pine tar in excess of the amount allowed in the rulebook. Home plate umpire Tim McClelland agreed, voiding the home run and calling Brett out, resulting in a Yankee victory. The Royals protested the game, and American League president Lee MacPhail overturned McClelland's ruling, forcing a resumption of the game at a later date, which resulted in a victory for the Royals.[5] But far more memorable than this victory is the image of Brett erupting from the dugout at the moment of McClelland's reversal, charging home plate, and being restrained by teammates and umpires who clearly feared for McClelland's safety. That visage of Brett's refusal to be denied what was rightfully his, right there on the home turf of the evil empire, has certainly done more to empower legions of Yankee haters than any regular season victory ever could. It's as if Brett had struck a blow against that empire; a system which, at that moment, seemed to reveal a seamy underbelly of collusion between Major League Baseball's supposedly impartial umpires and its most favored franchise.

While it was such a gesture by a single individual that allowed Cowhide to develop his own approach to dealing with the Yankees, other fans place the genesis of their Yankee hatred in that organization's treatment of two individuals within its own ranks, Casey Stengel and Joe Torre. Because Stengel served as manager for both the Yankees and the New York Mets, perhaps it is fitting that a fan known as Metman79 serves as the source of this cryptic observation: "I became a Mets fan partly because of my hatred for the Yankees and their dealings with Casey Stengel."[6] This appears to be a rather isolated complaint, and the historical record seems to contain little to warrant broader concern. Stengel, who managed the Yankees from 1949 to 1960, is arguably the most successful manager in Yankee history. After experiencing managerial success only at the minor-league level, he immediately led the Yankees to five consecutive World Series championships, adding five more American League pennants and two more World Series titles during his tenure. Given this record of success, Metman79's complaint is probably related to Stengel's firing after the Yankees' loss to the Pittsburgh Pirates in the 1960 World Series. Although Stengel was criticized for his management strategy during that series, it seems as if the main reason for his dismissal was his advanced age. As he commented to reporters after his firing, "I'll never make the mistake of being 70 again."[7] Perhaps Mets fans are uniquely sensitized to this age-related decision, as Stengel would become the manager of the newly formed franchise from 1962 to 1965. The Mets were so inept on the field of play that it was Stengel who served as the first object of affection for the new Mets fanbase. It appears that this affection continues to this day in the hearts of fans like Metman79.

As for Torre, his more recent dismissal as manager of the Yankees following the 2007 season has understandably resulted in more extensive fan comment. Washington Nationals fan ABryant hints at a karmic connection between Torre's firing and the fate of the evil empire in commenting that he is "so glad they are not playing well this year after treating Joe Torre the way they did last year. He was a class act and was a good reason they made the playoffs every year with him as manager."[8] Seeing something of a silver lining in Torre's firing, fellow Nationals fan Ericp331 claims, "It was more difficult to hate the Yankees when Torre was their manager. But now that he's in Los Angeles, it's easy again."[9] To some extent, Torre's role as the one thing about the Yankees that Yankee haters can endorse mirrors Stengel's role as the sole ray of light for Mets fans during those dismal early years. But letting Torre go only served to validate hatred of the Yankees organization, especially given the well-publicized conditions under which his dismissal occurred.

Torre's firing certainly came as no great surprise to baseball fans. Some speculated that Steinbrenner had been eager to oust Torre for years.[10] But when the Yankees fell to the Cleveland Indians in the 2007 American League Division Series, ensuring that the Yankees would fail to win the World Series for a seventh straight year, the consensus opinion was that Torre's fate was sealed. In fact, after losing the first two games of the series, Steinbrenner commented that Torre would probably not be asked to stay if the Yankees failed to advance.[11] At that point, a straightforward firing may have caused little consternation among fans. After all, in the midst of the Yankees' seven-year World Series drought, Torre received a three-year contract extension that made him the highest-paid manager in Major League Baseball. Not even the hot-headed Steinbrenner could be accused of acting irrationally by firing Torre; that's the kind of decision that team owners make all the time. But then, Steinbrenner chose to present a contract offer that many felt was designed to humiliate Torre and force him to leave voluntarily—a single year at $5 million, which was $2.5 million less than what he had earned in 2007, with a series of three $1 million performance incentives linked to postseason victories. Though he would have remained the highest-paid manager in the game, Torre declined the offer rather than accept the notion that, after leading the Yankees to four World Series championships and a playoff berth in each of his 12 seasons as manager, he should have to prove his worth to the organization. Compounding the perceived insult represented by this contract offer were comments made by Steinbrenner's son, Hank, who claimed that his father deserved the credit for making Torre a legend in New York Yankee history. While maintaining his respectful opinion of the Yankees' owner, Torre claimed that the younger Steinbrenner simply did not understand the competitive nature of baseball. According to Torre, "the insult came from the incentive-based situation, and unless you understand what sport is all about and how important winning is to you, I don't think you understand the insult part of this thing. I don't think incentives are necessary. I've

been here a long time and I've never needed to be motivated."[12] Despite
Torre's unflinching gratitude for the opportunity given to him by the elder
Steinbrenner, some felt that the Yankees' owner disliked Torre because
he received too much credit for the Yankees' success and was overpaid.[13]
That's right, the man who saw fit to pay a record-setting $200 million to
a team he considered a failure thought the manager who led that team to
12 consecutive postseason appearances was overpaid. Perhaps Spastic,
an Atlanta Braves fan, sums it up as well as anyone could by claiming
"they're just a classless organization with a classless owner."[14]

Understandably more concerned with the fortunes of their team than
with those of any manager, Yankees fans trolling the message boards had
little to say on the matter. But the fans of those other 29 teams had found a
cause célèbre to fuel their Yankee hatred. Torre's kind words notwithstanding, he and Casey Stengel had become innocent victims of the empire, and
the current human face of that empire belongs to the owner of the Yankees,
George Steinbrenner. While he may simply be one owner among 30, it is
difficult for fans to see him as something other than first among equals; as
a man who often seems to call the shots to a greater degree than the Commissioner's Office, whose undue influence on Major League Baseball's
fortunes is inextricably linked to his own personal fortune. It is this personal fortune that provides the current justification for what is perhaps the
most common complaint about the Yankees' contribution to this diabolical
system: they buy championships.

Of course, this complaint about the influence of the Yankees' wealth
does not begin and end with Steinbrenner's wallet. In his 2004 book, titled
Imperial America, Gore Vidal mocks what he sees as the American lack
of regard for the importance of history by invoking the phrase "the United
States of Amnesia" in the book's subtitle. At first blush, it may seem that
Yankee hatred aimed at Steinbrenner's recent tenure as owner stands as
good evidence that baseball fans have fallen prey to such historical amnesia. But the following exchange between two supporters of the Chicago
White Sox indicates that not all fans are blind to the influence of Yankee
dollars in the pre-Steinbrenner era:

[Wsoxrock writes] I think it's ridiculous to hate the Yankees for their history. Twenty-seven World Series is just too much to have any jealousy for.
That deserves respect, especially since most World Series appearances were
before payrolls skyrocketed, during days when the playing field was more
level.[15]

[Chgophil replies] While you are correct in stating that all but six of the
Yankees' titles came before free agency, the Yankees always took advantage
of playing in the largest media market. Didn't the Yankees acquire Babe
Ruth from the Red Sox for nothing but cash?[16]

First, I guess Chgophil deserves some credit here for resisting any impulse to correct Wsoxrock for suggesting that the Yankees have 27 World Series titles (they've appeared in 39 World Series and won 26) and focusing on a more substantive aspect of historical amnesia. Babe Ruth was, in fact, purchased by the Yankees from the Red Sox on January 3, 1920, for the sum of $100,000.[17] While Wsoxrock would be correct to situate this deal prior to the era of high player salaries ushered in by free agency, the Yankees did double the $10,000 salary paid to Ruth by the Red Sox in 1919.[18] But even if we ignore concerns about inflated salaries, the Babe Ruth deal reeks of influence purchased by New York money. Red Sox Owner Harry Frazee had accumulated his wealth as a Broadway producer, and kept an office in New York's Frazee Theater a mere two blocks from the offices of the Yankees. One of his drinking companions was a co-owner of the Yankees, who apparently saw an opportunity when Frazee's finances were damaged by the strain placed on the entertainment industry by World War I.[19] So, it appears that the level playing field assumed by Wsoxrock had room for a pair of New Yorkers arranging a deal in which the superior wealth of Yankees ownership would capitalize on another team owner's financial hardship, followed by four World Series victories for the Yankees over the following 13 seasons and a championship drought for the Red Sox lasting into the following century. Now, if historical amnesia were accompanied by the assumption that baseball's distant past was governed by the same financial imperative cited in the living present, perhaps that amnesia wouldn't be considered such a problem.

The recent combination of free agency and Steinbrenner's millions has left little doubt in the minds of baseball fans as to the current effect of this financial imperative. Simply put, the rich Yankees get richer, while most of the 29 other comparatively poor teams get poorer. This reductionist interpretation is reflected in Cleveland Indians fan Roger Dorn's answer to the question of why he hates the Yankees: "Buying championships, not building teams. It's as simple as that."[20] Others, like Colorado Rockies fan Freejamsociety, apply a more nuanced analysis grounded in socioeconomic theories that transcend the diamond:

> It is simply a traditional and "richly" deserved resentment of the excessively wealthy. In an age in which greedy, billionaire multinationalists, along with their all too willing accomplices in the military-industrial complex, are rapidly enslaving the entire planet, this is to be entirely expected.[21]

For some, like Baltimore Orioles fan Schwender7, it seems that it is size that matters the most:

> The Yankees have always bought up the best players out of free agency to go to the World Series time and time again. This is due in part to being

located in one of the most populous cities in the world. With a 16 million-person market to cater to (meanwhile, the city of Baltimore has 700,000), they make the money and can afford to splurge on big-name players. This is, in effect, buying championships. If money had been an even playing field since baseball's inception, teams like the Yankees would have considerably less championships and considerably less fans, making them considerably less obnoxious.[22]

And others, like Philadelphia Phillies fan Jcballer, take a kitchen-sink approach aimed not only at the competitive advantage created by the Yankees' wealth, but also at the affect that wealth has on the more modest finances of the average fan:

> The Yankees go against everything that I love about Major League Baseball. They completely defeat the arguments of, "Do you keep this prospect, or trade for the veteran player who could put you over the top?" They completely remove front office strategy. Their offseason doesn't present, "Do we spend $10 million here or $5 million on these two?" Their answer is always, "Well, let's just spend $20 million and get them all." As a true lover of the sport and of the strategy and planning that goes into running a team that can't have a $220 million payroll, I don't know how you can possibly cheer for them. They singlehandedly create an argument for the salary cap. They inflate free agent and draftee salaries. They, as one organization, are the reason why my ticket prices in Philly have to keep going up.[23]

Finally, there are those, like Los Angeles Angels of Anaheim fan CalifCajun, who don't really hate the Yankees, but simply can't abide Steinbrenner as a person:

> I don't like economic disparity and loudmouth owners that run the game's most storied franchise into the ground. The Angels are operated in a more professional manner than the Yankees are. I don't hate the Yankees. I wish they would clean up their act.[24]

For a few like CalifCajun, it seems that just getting rid of Steinbrenner would cure their Yankee hatred. But for most, Steinbrenner is simply the current manifestation of the big-money advantage that the Yankees have always enjoyed. It is that institutional financial clout, rather than any evil motive from within even the most distasteful owner, that Major League Baseball just can't help but favor.

There is a fairly strong sentiment among fans that the problem of financial inequality in Major League Baseball, which often results in hatred of the Yankees, is actually due to the policies of Major League Baseball itself. As the most profitable individual franchise in the professional baseball industry, the Yankees may simply be getting the blame due to the organization's high visibility among fans. After all, reacting negatively to an on-field presence seems far more convenient than assessing the negative impact of league policy. In this way, perhaps the Yankee hatred based on financial advantage is a case of "blaming the on-field messenger," when the blame should be on those who manage the conditions under which the message is structured. According to most of the fans who express this sentiment, the central dichotomy resulting in this problem of financial inequality is the big market versus small market dynamic. Not surprisingly, the vast majority of fans concerned with this issue are found on the message boards of small-market teams like the Pittsburgh Pirates, on which the following discussion developed:

> [Cpt Jack writes] It is because of the Yankees and other large spending teams that it is almost impossible for the Pirates to draft the best player in the game and keep him his entire career . . . Roberto Clemente would have left the Pirates as a free agent if he played today. [Barry] Bonds left. The system makes it difficult for all-time greats to stay with the team that drafts them. It also makes it impossible for the Pirates or other small-spending teams to be good for more than a few years at a time. The Yankees can be good and go to the playoffs for more than a decade. When they have a hole to fill, they buy a free agent. The current system is built for the large cities to have a huge advantage. The Yankees like it that way because it allows them a better chance to win every year and make more money. They don't care about the game or the fans in the little cities like Pittsburgh. And then, when teams like the Pirates and Rays struggle for years, they say it's not their fault, that you guys just don't know how to make good baseball decisions. Why should the big cities, especially New York, be the center of the baseball universe? What, New York fans are more important than Pittsburgh fans? Yeah, they do all they can to win, while other cities suffer. I guess the sooner I learn that New Yorkers are superior to Pittsburghers and deserve all of the finest things in life, I guess the happier I will be.[25]

> [Fla pirate replies] You are right. We don't have $200 million to spend, but we do receive money/welfare from MLB [Major League Baseball]. The problem we have is that we were bleeding dollars the last time we were competitive. Our financial situation is much better with a new stadium, but we have failed to deliver a winning team in a long time. Part of that is cheapness from Bob [Nutting, Pirates owner], part of it was bad trades by DL [Dave Littlefield, Pirates General Manager from 2001–07], and part of that was lousy free agent/drafting by DL and Bob. Now, we don't have the Yankee luxury of being able to buy an All-Star roster replacement for our team, so we have to do it the long, hard way of drafting and trading talent. If we suddenly found a winning team, ticket sales would go up, and merchandise sales would be up, and magically, we would have more to sign and

lock up better players. Since we have the opposite situation, our revenues keep going down and, as Goose pointed out in another thread, it gives Bob the excuse to not spend money, because why waste more money on a downward spiraling team. So, large cities have a big advantage, and our margin for error is small.[26]

[Cpt Jack replies] The NBA [National Basketball Association], NHL [National Hockey League], and NFL [National Football League] all respect and give the smaller-market teams a chance to win and build dynasties. There is a reason that Jacksonville, Columbus, Indianapolis, and Portland have teams in those leagues. Those leagues value smaller cities and give them a chance. MLB has decided to emphasize the larger cities. Their revenue and attendance keep going up, so maybe they are doing the right thing. But I don't agree with that.[27]

[Accuscore replies] I used to hate the Yankees for a lot of the reasons mentioned, mainly the arrogant fans and the way they buy championships. Then, a few things happened. Boston started buying championships, their fans got arrogant, and I started siding with Yankees fans. I realized that the "buying championships" problem was not the fault of the Yankees, it was MLB's fault. MLB is designed to favor teams like the Yankees. What are they supposed to do, willingly give up their advantage because it is unfair? It's the job of MLB to make things fair, and it's the Yankees' job to win within the rules that MLB provides.[28]

[Cecenation replies] Cpt Jack, you're right, but you have the wrong culprit. It's not the Yanks who have turned their backs on the small markets. It's the MLB. I can't blame the Yanks for this flawed system. Each club should be able to act in its own best interests to field the best possible team. It's the MLB's fault for not setting boundaries and restrictions that would make it a more competitive and equitable system.[29]

[Cpt Jack replies] Let's face it. The Pirates are in Pittsburgh because they started there over a hundred years ago. Pittsburgh would never have gotten a team through expansion. It is only a matter of time before the Pirates move. It won't be soon, but at some point, the demographics will not support a MLB team. Every year, Pittsburgh is losing population and other cities continue to grow. Let's hope MLB can change the economics to allow the Pirates to stay in a smaller city. I doubt it, though. Whenever the lease at PNC Park is up, they might leave. I won't blame them under the current system.[30]

[Mongoose replies] You're learning, Captain.[31]

What began with Cpt Jack's vigorous complaint about the Yankees and other big-market teams preventing the Pirates from retaining their best players quickly developed into a discussion focused on a bigger problem in this system: Major League Baseball itself. The lesson that Cpt Jack supposedly learns by the end of the discussion is cloaked in the sadness and resignation felt by many fans of small-market teams when confronted with the realization that this system simply can't work for them.

Perhaps emboldened by this realization that the problem might be driven by Major League Baseball and not the Yankees, some Yankees fans ventured into these discussions and attempted to repair the organization's reputation when the rare opportunity to do so presented itself:

[Yanksfan53 writes] Most of the championships they [the Yankees] won were with homegrown players. It's only been the last seven years or so when they started trying to buy championships. But half of their '08 roster came out of the farm system, so that's changing.[32]

[Roger Dorn replies] They cancel out free agent signings for teams like the Indians because players know they can always get that extra 2–3 million per year by going to another team. Boston has become the exact same way. It's the reason why Manny Ramirez isn't an Indian anymore, and won't go into the Hall of Fame in a Tribe uniform.[33]

[Yanksfan53 replies] I know, but it seems like many small-market teams are trying to stop that from happening by signing their players before they reach free agent status. The Indians have done it with [outfielder Grady] Sizemore and [pitcher Fausto] Carmona; the Rays have done it with [third baseman Evan] Longoria, [pitcher Scott] Kazmir, [pitcher James] Shields, and [first baseman Carlos] Pena; and the Marlins have done it with Hanley Ramirez.[34]

[Red 1 replies] That doesn't really change much for a small-market team. When they sign their players like Sizemore and Carmona, it's usually only through their arbitration years anyway when they can't leave anyhow, with maybe an extra year or two added on if the small-market team is really lucky. They still end up going to free agency and we can't afford them long term. It's exactly why we're going to lose [pitcher C.C.] Sabathia after this season. It's why the Twins lost [outfielder Torii] Hunter and [pitcher Johan] Santana last offseason. We are forced to try and replace them with prospects. The problem with that is you have a couple of bad years in the draft and you're screwed. We even have a disadvantage when it comes to the draft because of the huge signing bonuses the big-market teams throw at these kids who have never played before. If they're a really hot prospect, a lot of small-market teams have to skip over them in the draft no matter how badly they want them because they know they can't sign them now. So, even in developing from within, you have a huge advantage.[35]

Yes, that's the same Roger Dorn, fan of the small-market Cleveland Indians that we heard from earlier, weighing in here. Although Yanksfan53 offers up his best defense in a respectful manner, these small-market fans are having none of it. The tide of events seems to support their position, as Red 1's prediction of the Indians' loss of C.C. Sabathia actually came true *before* the end of the 2008 season. Still, overt expression of Yankee hatred is largely absent here, the implication being that the structure and policies of Major League Baseball are the real culprits.

However, a discussion that emerged on the small-market Oakland A's message boards indicates an awareness among some fans that Major League Baseball has not always facilitated this big-market advantage:

[Raptorman writes] It would be one thing if the Yankees bought everyone's talent and were continually in the World Series. However, they haven't won the Series for quite some time, but have driven everyone else's payroll costs through the roof and ruined the game for smaller-market teams in the process. IMO [in my opinion], the Yankees' current woes are entirely self-inflicted and overdue. They're a mediocre team (at best) with not a lot of talent in the pipeline.[36]

[Salbando6 replies] Raptorman, I have to disagree with you. Yes, the Yankees have done their part but, really, the fault lies with [current Commissioner of Major League Baseball] Bud Selig. When Charlie [Finley, former A's owner and General Manager] sold [outfielder Joe] Rudi and [pitcher Rollie] Fingers to the Red Sox (and [pitcher] Vida [Blue] to the Yanks), Bowie Kuhn [Commissioner from 1969–84] stepped in and voided the deals as he felt they were not "in the best interests of baseball." Do you think Bud would do that today? Heck, no! Bud is the reason that there is such a wide margin between the haves and have-nots. In the past . . . , the Yankees would spend, spend, spend, but the game had a way of correcting itself. Now, since Bud, he has single-handedly "convinced" owners that the only way they can make money is with a new ballpark, which automatically raises ticket prices, etc. Small-market teams don't work as well, but as you notice, there are still new ballparks in Pittsburgh, Detroit, and Cincinnati (with "in the works" parks in Oakland, Minnesota, and others). We will probably still disagree, but the original A-Rod [Alex Rodriguez] deal with Texas was really the harbinger of the current free agent market. And who paid that money to A-Rod? Why, Texas, of course, with their new ballpark revenue, which Bud then used to "sell" the other owners . . . : "See the new ballpark? Isn't it nice? See their newest star? You can have (buy) an A-Rod, too, if you get a new ballpark." See, if it was just George [Steinbrenner], how could you explain the A's of 1988–92? George owned the Yankees, but Bud was not the commish at that time. Oh, the A's of 2000-present? Bud was/is commissioner in that time. How do I explain that? Easy. Only the super-creative and brilliant [A's General Manager] Billy Beane has been able to keep the A's competitive. But the key word is "creative." Every year, there are less and less "name" players on the A's. That is not Billy's choice. That is Billy somehow filling the A's gas tank year after year with the same $20, even though it costs everyone else $50.[37]

[Raptorman replies] The Yankmees [Yankees] started a fire they can't put out (i.e., overpaying underperforming stupid stars). That's not to say they broke any rules. They took advantage of the rules and commissioners of baseball making the rules at the time. I agree with one of your points—Selig is a bigger idiot than Kuhn, Fay Vincent [Commissioner from 1989–92], and Bart G [A. Bartlett Giamatti, Commissioner prior to Vincent during the 1989 season] put together.[38]

Well, at least these two can agree on something! Following the familiar pattern displayed in the previous discussion among Pirates fans, Raptor-man enters the fray prepared to eviscerate the evil empire of the Yankees, only to open a rather nuanced dialogue regarding not only the structure of the baseball industry, but also the shortcomings of the most recent occupant of the Commissioner's Office. Clearly, there appears to be a willingness on the part of fans to place blame for the system's failures on those who dwell at the apex of that system. It's Major League Baseball's world; the Yankees, though worthy of hatred, are just living in it. However, there may be a force at work here that eclipses the evil done by either the Yankees or Major League Baseball; an institution that has achieved such complete hegemony over our lives that its influence appears, at first blush, to be part of the forces of nature. But trust the fans not to leave even this stone unturned.

While a full consideration of the contribution of media coverage to the dominance of the Yankees is beyond the scope of this writing, it is a phenomenon that did not escape the attention of fans as they attempted to explain their Yankee hatred. Fan discussions about the role of media coverage in the development of this hated system often begin with an attempt to locate a point of origin in baseball's brief history as a televised sport, which corresponds temporally to the distant childhood memories of many fans. The following exchange between Washington Nationals fans provides a good example:

[ericp331 writes] Historically, the reason so many fans hate the Yankees was because in the 1950s and 1960s, pretty much every TV game of the week was a Yankees game, in large part because CBS owned the Yankees at the time. That's also why so many fans are Yankees fans, because if they didn't have their own team to root for, who was on TV with all the stars and always winning? And, thanks to FOX from 1995 on, it's been more wall-to-wall Yankees adulation by [announcers] Joe Buck and Tim McCarver. So, another generation of Yankees fans.[39]

[RayD replies] I don't think that's historically accurate. The great Yankee dynasty of that period ran from the late 40s ('48 or '49) through 1964. CBS bought them, as I recall, in 1964, one of the most ill-timed business transactions in history. By 1965, the Yankees were one of the worst teams in the American League, and never resurfaced until the mid-70s. No, I think the reason they were on TV during the 50s through 1964 is that they were America's team and that's who everyone wanted to see. I remember going to [Washington] Senators games during that period, and attendance tripled when the Yankees were here—not from local fans, nor New York fans, but from the South (North Carolina, etc.) and the West.[40]

Well, score one for RayD here on the grounds of historical accuracy. On November 2, 1964, CBS purchased a controlling interest in the Yankees for $11.2 million.[41] It is true that prior to the sale of the Yankees to CBS, the ownership team of Dan Topping, Del Webb, and Larry MacPhail presided over a 20-year dynasty that saw the Yankees win 10 of 15 World Series appearances. In contrast, the Yankees saw not a single World Series during eight seasons of CBS ownership, finishing in last place in 1966 for the first time since 1912. So, prior to 1964, it seems that the media dominance of the Yankees is more attributable to their stellar play on the field than any sinister collusion with the broadcasting industry. Despite his somewhat more accurate timeline regarding FOX as a baseball broadcaster, Ericp331 fails to acknowledge that much of that dreaded televised adulation of the Yankees in recent years may have been due to the Yankees' on-field prowess, which has resulted in 13 consecutive postseason appearances since 1995.

But Yankee on-field dynasties notwithstanding, Ericp331's complaint about the Yankees dominating the spectator ritual of a nationally televised weekly game is not without merit. Before the 1964 sale of the Yankees to CBS, Major League Baseball's agreement with television broadcasters allocated payments to teams based on the number of times each team appeared in a national telecast. Perhaps due to their status as the best team in baseball since the game became a televised spectacle, the Yankees led the list of revenue-generating appearances. But once CBS became the owner of the Yankees, this lucrative symbiotic relationship began to resemble an open conflict of interest in which CBS would actually be paying itself every time a Yankees game hit the airwaves. In 1965, in order to avoid the continued appearance of impropriety, Major League Baseball adopted the practice of distributing television revenue equally among all teams. By doing so during a period of growing television revenue, Major League Baseball actually ushered in an era of enhanced competitive balance due to greater economic parity.[42] Still, the perception of the Yankees as an overbearing presence in televised baseball persists in the consciousness of many fans. That perception seems amplified by the idea that this media dominance could continue, even as the Yankees entered a period of mediocrity, simply because of an ownership connection to the television industry:

When CBS bought the Yanks in the mid-60s, the one national weekly Saturday TV game became the Yankee game of the week. At that point, pretty much all fans of any other team hated the Yankees. The Steinbrenner era of "just buy the players you need" just further cemented the emotion. Yes, there are Indians, Orioles, and Braves fans in my family in addition to myself as the lone White Sox fan, and the one thing we share is hatred of the Yankees. The fact that the national media dotes on them and always has doesn't help either.[43]

This comment from Trademarc1 indicates that the position of the Yankees as undeserving media darlings while under CBS ownership was merely one developmental stage in the widespread phenomenon of Yankee hatred. The dawn of the Steinbrenner era would introduce a revised list of reasons to hate the Yankees, including the manipulation of media power.

One might think that purchasing the Yankees while their on-field fortunes were at a low ebb would generate some degree of sympathy for George Steinbrenner. After all, he purchased the club from CBS in January of 1973 for a mere $10 million—less than CBS paid almost a decade earlier.[44] But any grace period that could be accorded to the new owner on the basis of nonthreatening team performance quickly evaporated, as the Yankees returned to postseason play only four seasons later. The influence of media exposure and the revenue it generates certainly played a part in the resurgence of Yankee hatred that accompanied this return to success. The Yankees had always been the pioneering franchise regarding the generation of income from television, having cut the first local television deal in Major League Baseball in 1946.[45] But the impact of such deals during the television industry's infancy was minimal compared to the effect of the Yankees' media dominance during the Steinbrenner era. Beginning in the early 1990s, the Yankees' local cable television contract provided the foundation for the franchise's superior financial position relative to other teams which, in response, sought to emulate this model on a more modest scale. Unfortunately for those other teams, this increased reliance on local cable television revenue coincided with the dissolution of the national television broadcasting contract and, along with it, Major League Baseball's practice of equally distributing television revenue among all teams. What ensued was a new era of decreasing financial equality, with big-market teams like the Yankees rising to positions of financial dominance. This would account for much of the money-based Yankee hatred expressed by fans during the Yankees' most recent championship dynasty under Steinbrenner's ownership. But what would account for hatred of Steinbrenner and his Yankees in the early years, prior to the advent of unequal local cable television dollars? Wouldn't fans consider the Yankees' late-1970s success under more equitable financial circumstances to be somehow more acceptable? Not quite. According to White Sox fan Chgophil, the Yankees' status as the biggest of big-market teams trumps any consideration of ownership style, media technology, or financial distribution scheme:

> The Yankees' success is not due to a superior business model, but rather to an inherently more profitable broadcast market. They make more money from radio than some teams make from television, and their fans have come to believe that living in the larger city entitles them to players that fans in smaller cities can only dream of. This disparity is exacerbated by the national networks' fixation on the East Coast teams, causing the small-minded masses around the nation to decide to become Yankee "fans."[46]

This big-market advantage of naturally abundant media dollars would not only cause Yankee haters to target George Steinbrenner; it would also provide them with a new focus in the person of his son, Hank, who recently dared to become a media voice. The following parenthetical chat between two Washington Nationals fans can be considered an early warning to the younger Steinbrenner about the cost of the free expression of ideas by those associated with the Yankees:

> [Zilla2005 writes] Well, now Hank is a "columnist" for the *Sporting News*. I guess we really need a column defending his version of "Moneyball"— spending $200 million for an aging lineup.[47]
>
> [Ericp331 replies] He's a "columnist," not just writing an op-ed? Great. Glad I don't subscribe to the *Sporting News*, if they feel the need to be the Yankees' bullhorn.[48]

This brief exchange suggests that any media linkage to the source of Yankee hatred goes beyond griping about the financial advantage created by operating in the nation's largest local media market. Just as prevalent are fan complaints regarding a perceived East Coast bias in national media coverage of the sport. The aforementioned decline of over-the-air baseball broadcasting in the 1990s not only enabled the rise of local cable television coverage of the game, but it also fueled a market for national cable coverage as American homes increasingly bought in to cable technology. Since its launch in 1979, ESPN was uniquely situated as the primary purveyor of sports programming on cable at the national level, having grown along with the cable industry through the 1980s and into the 1990s. So, it should come as no surprise that ESPN would become a prime media focus uniting Yankee haters nationwide in an "East Coast versus The Rest of Us" struggle. In the opinion of Chicago Cubs fan Jono3, it is this East Coast bias of the national media that serves as the primary fuel for generating Yankee hatred:

> The most hate comes from all the coverage the Yankees get . . . I'm so sick of the media thinking East Coast teams are the most important.[49]

Angels fan Rds1 dispenses with the notion of hating the Yankees altogether, placing the onus solely on ESPN:

> I may not like some of their fanbase, and I'm tired of hearing about Red Sox Nation and the love ESPN has for the Sox, Yankees, and anything "eastern." But other than ESPN's lopsided coverage, I have no hatred.[50]

A discussion among Cardinals fans revealed a more detailed version of this viewpoint:

> [Sirphobos writes] I don't hate the Yankees. I hate how ESPN thinks the Red Sox and Yankees are the only two teams in Major League Baseball that matter. The [Yankees pitcher] Joba Chamberlain thing is a prime example. Who cares that he's making his first starts? Did [Cardinals pitcher Adam] Wainwright get this kind of national attention when he moved to being a starter? He did a lot more as a reliever than Joba did.[51]
>
> [Hess replies] I don't hate the Yankees, per se. The thing is, I don't really care about them one way or the other. I'm simply tired of the Yankees, and of the Red Sox, for that matter. I'm tired of their dominance of national media coverage. I don't really care about either team, yet I hear about them constantly. I know as much about them as I do about the team I actually root for. I resent that, therefore I resent them. I just want them to fade into the background like other teams I don't root for and not be shoved down my throat constantly.[52]

It's worth noting that these complaints about an East Coast bias come from fans of a big-market team in the Midwest, a big-market team on the West Coast, and a small-market team in the Midwest. While it's understandable that none were gleaned from the message boards of East Coast teams, it's difficult to locate a factor common to these complaints beyond the fact that they are generated somewhere other than the East Coast. Is this a "Chicago versus New York" big city rivalry, an "East Coast versus West Coast" feud, or an "urban center versus fly-over country" culture war? Are we even talking about Yankee hatred here? Or is Yankee hatred simply a resentment of East Coast media bias by proxy? This ambivalence among fans regarding hatred of both the Yankees and East Coast media bias points to larger questions regarding precisely what aspect of this hated system really merits all this hatred.

In his list of rules to be followed by mature, reasonable sports fans who "know the score," author, humorist, and sports fan Joe Queenan tops off the list with an entry labeled, "Stop bitching about the Yankees," in which he provides this sage advice:

> When push comes to shove, moaning and groaning about the Yankees hegemony is like complaining about August humidity or the *New York Times'*

liberal bias. They are forces of nature; stop banging your head against the wall . . . You only have to be a fan for about four months before you realize that even when something great happens to your team, it is probably not going to be remembered because it didn't happen in New York.[53]

Of course, Queenan's call for an end to futile complaints about the Yankees is immediately followed by several pages of his own complaints about the Yankees; complaints about insufferable celebrity Yankee fan Billy Crystal, Lou Gehrig's overexposed "luckiest man in the world" speech, and the absurdity of supporters of the routinely victorious Yankees describing themselves as "die-hard fans." Yet, Queenan's own ambivalence is redeemed by his observation that fans derive something positive from all the negativity of Yankee hatred:

> They remind us that life is not fair, that some are born to sweet delight, some are born to endless night. The Yanks, omnipotent deities, win all the time as they're supposed to win. More power to them. But there's no poetry in their victories. They have a huge checkbook. They open it. But Yankees fans trying to trade old war stories bring to mind the scene in *Cobb*, where the aging Georgia Peach gets refused entrance to a private Cooperstown party filled to overflowing with the lions of the game. Sorry, guys, us ordinary fans from Detroit and Cincinnati are busy discussing blown pennants, false springs, good riddance, bad trades. We don't want you in here. You don't have standing.[54]

While most fan narratives of Yankee hatred lack Queenan's eloquence, many embody the same sort of ambivalence with a silver lining. If your team can't get it done on the field, then maybe some shred of dignity can be salvaged through a celebration of the strength required to cheer for a loser. It's not a terribly exclusive club, but at least it excludes the Yankees and their followers. That measure of dignified exclusivity seems to open up some space for charitable discourse within this universe of hatred for the Yankees' evil empire and the system that supports it. Amazingly, one focus for this occasional beneficence is the Evil One himself, George Steinbrenner. NYCanito, a native New Yorker who relocated to South Florida and became a Marlins fan before moving back to New York and deciding to split his allegiance between the Mets and the Marlins (talk about ambivalence!), offers the following statement, which typifies this unexpected magnanimity:

> Most people hate the Yankees because they have an owner with money who cares about the team and puts the money back on the field. Even if they don't win, they are committed to and get what they need . . . I am not a Yankee fan, but I wish we had an owner like the Yankees.[55]

An even more surprising kindness is offered by Theroostah, who resides in the most ardent of Yankee-hating fanbases: that of the Boston Red Sox:

> Oddly enough, I bear no malice toward Steinbrenner, Sr. While I'm not exactly a fan, I have to give the guy credit for his dedication to try to win. I saw him in an interview awhile ago regarding the high salaries in baseball, and he said that he doesn't want to pay a lot of money any more than anyone else, but he feels he owes it to the NY fans to give them the best team possible. Now, whether that's his only motive, or whether big name players also generate interest in the Yankees, is beside the point. The main thing is that he always puts a contending team on the field, as does the triumvirate of [Red Sox owners] Henry-Lucchino-Werner and, frankly, I think that's great. If all an owner can do is have a perennial bottom-feeder, they should be in some other business.[56]

Of course, the love-hate ambivalence in fans' opinions about the Yankees' owner is bound to rise to the surface eventually, as it does in this comment from Pittsburgh Pirates fan Fla pirate:

> I hate the fact that they can buy an All-Star roster each year and thumb their nose at the luxury tax. I hate the fact that baseball revolves around the Yankees and Mets because New York City is the center of the baseball world. They should just give the Yankees the trophy every year and not worry about a playoff series. It would cut down the season by a month. I hate the fact that their owner cares so much more about winning than ours and isn't afraid to call out his players and coaches when they aren't performing. I hate the Yankees because they have managed to be our polar opposite for the last 15 years.[57]

This rather open expression of jealousy, erupting from a laundry list of reasons to hate the Yankees, may lend a bit of credence to the French saying, "Love expels jealousy." If so, perhaps the ambivalence we are detecting here is not really love-hate ambivalence. Perhaps we're mistaking jealousy for love. Perhaps Pittsburgh has more in common with Paris than any of us ever imagined. In any case, a less thorny reaction to expressions of hatred for the Yankees' owner comes from Chicago White Sox fan BeerMan58, who puts an end to the debate by opining, "Steinbrenner is great on *Seinfeld*, though."[58]

At times, this ambivalent fan sentiment regarding the Yankees' owner extends to the entire organization, as demonstrated in this post from Pirates fan Doc hamp:

> I don't hate the Yankees. I know that people do hate them for various reasons—the money they spend, George Steinbrenner, their long tradition

of winning—but I think those are mostly sour grapes reasons. The Yankees are simply doing what they can, the way the rules are structured today, to win.[59]

Some, like Pirates fan Srs5020, are fully aware of the evolution of their own ambivalence regarding Yankee hatred:

I can honestly say that I used to be one of the many baseball fans who hated the Yankees with a passion, primarily because they went out and bought big name free agents year in and year out. But, they are playing by the rules. Nothing in baseball says that they can't go out and buy whoever they want every year. The Yankees' front office has a passion to win and win now, and that is something that I respect greatly.[60]

Others, like Chicago Cubs fan Movelli, are a bit less self-reflective about the matter:

Who cares if they pay for their championships? Not their fault they have the money![61]

But this willingness to excuse the Yankees' dominance because they're just following the rules of Major League Baseball does have its limits. Some fans interpret the Yankees' position of financial power not as a license to dominate the game through profligate spending, but as a call to exercise responsibility for mending a broken system:

[Cpt Jack writes] The Yankees can work to change the system. I have a lot of respect for the owners of the New York football Giants. They worked with other teams in the league to create a system that allowed the Steelers to compete and win Super Bowls. The Giants gave up some of their advantage in money to help build the league . . . With a little help and leadership from the large revenue teams, MLB could have a salary cap. They would need to share some more revenue and put in a salary floor. Done right, the players will actually have a bigger pool of money for salary . . . This system would give every team a much better chance to compete year in and year out. I see the players resistant to such a plan, but I also see the Yankees and Red Sox, etc., against such an idea. They don't want to give up their advantage in revenue.[62]

[Accuscore replies] The Giants made that call when free agency first came around. It was a big concession, but it was easier back in the 70s. It would be nearly impossible for baseball to make that kind of change now. If they installed a salary cap and revenue sharing, how would teams like the Yankees and Red Sox get under the cap?[63]

The idea of using a salary cap as an instrument for leveling the financial playing field resonates with past attempts to control the economic structure of the game. In addition, it still offers a ray of hope for those fans torn by a desire for fairness and an admiration of the athletic excellence that a team with money can buy. But the history of those past attempts designed to ameliorate economic imbalances is spotty, at best. After all, if they achieved that desired effect, would fans still be complaining?

In any spectator sport, a central attraction for fans is the feature that might be termed *problematic outcome*, or uncertainty over just which competitor will eventually emerge victorious. But if fans are routinely offered contests between unevenly matched competitors, the outcome of those contests will become predictable and boring. This condition is, of course, bad for spectator attendance and bad for the business of sports. Achieving competitive balance in spectator sports is, therefore, something that fans, team owners, and league administrators value highly, and preventing large differences in the wealth of individual teams is an obvious way to get there. Not surprisingly, the history of professional baseball is replete with attempts to ensure against fans losing interest in a sure loser or becoming complacent about supporting a sure winner. Perhaps the first such attempt was the National League's introduction of the reserve clause in 1879. An open restraint of trade predating the Sherman Antitrust Act, the reserve clause represents an attempt to halt the escalation of player salaries resulting from their migration from poorer clubs to wealthier ones. By allowing teams to reserve the services of a core of players from one year to the next, the league sought to maintain a competitive balance on the field that would result in enhanced financial prospects for the league as a whole. As might be expected, the introduction of the reserve clause ignited a classic battle between management's desire for competitive balance and labor's desire to freely bargain for maximum compensation for services rendered on the field of play. This battle would periodically rage in court cases and legislative hearings until the repeal of the reserve clause and the advent of free agency in the 1970s, ushering in the current era of players free to sell their services to the highest bidder. But the question remains: Is competitive balance even affected by the imposition or removal of the reserve clause? It's difficult to say. After all, there's plenty of evidence that valuable players will wind up playing for wealthy big-market teams with or without the reserve clause. Recall that Babe Ruth became a Yankee under the reserve clause simply by virtue of one owner selling him to another for cash. It's difficult to argue that those Yankee dynasties of the reserve-clause era stand as greater symbols of competitive balance than the shorter-lived dynasties of the 1970s and 1990s. Can fans reasonably expect schemes involving salary caps to achieve better results? Has Major League Baseball's luxury tax, imposed on the wealthiest clubs and happily paid by teams like the Yankees, resulted in enhanced competitive balance? Or has the cost of that tax been easily absorbed by the Yankees' inherently more profitable broadcast market and what have been cited as "perverse incentives in baseball's revenue sharing system," which seem to work against the small-market teams that revenue sharing is intended to help?[64] Even if salary caps, salary floors, or other instruments were added to the mix of measures designed to achieve a level financial playing field, is Accuscore correct in his claim that it might just be too late for Major League Baseball to fix its broken system? With such a varied past and an equally uncertain future, ambivalent feelings about that system seem understandable and inevitable.

This ambivalence is manifest in areas that transcend Steinbrenner, the Yankees, the media, and the Commissioner's Office. A favorite whipping boy for those who lament the uncontrolled influence of money in the sport has been the Major League Baseball Players Association. Surprisingly, negative fan commentary about the role this union plays in the development of Yankee hatred in particular, or system hatred in general, was relatively sparse, and any criticism of it tended to be accompanied by a cast of supporting evil doers:

> I blame three groups for not having a salary cap in baseball. The number one reason is the players union. They will fight it to the end. Number two is the large revenue teams like the Yankees. They benefit from the current system, so why change it. They always say the same thing: "We are just following the rules." I say the rules are biased towards them and they see no reason to change them. They are not innocent in how small revenue teams are treated in MLB. They could stand up with all owners and demand a cap. They won't, and then they will hide behind "We are just following the rules," and "We want to win more than anyone else," and "Why should we give money to other teams?" Finally I blame the agents. A few super-agents that represent the best players make more money under this system. They don't care that under a floor and cap the middle class or lower level guy will make more money. They only care about their top clients.[65]

It's noteworthy that, of the three reasons given here by Cpt Jack for the absence of a salary cap in Major League Baseball, the players union receives short shrift. Perhaps this is due to his belief that the case against the union is an obvious one that requires little explanation, or maybe it is due to the realization that the salary issue most directly affected by the Players Association is the league minimum paid to those relatively impoverished athletes at the bottom of the pay scale. But whatever the reason, his most detailed criticisms are reserved for player agents and wealthy teams like the Yankees: elite actors at the apex of the sport's financial pyramid that could change things if they truly cared to do so.

Another source of ambivalence toward this supposedly unjust system may stem from the World Series victory drought experienced by the Yankees after 2000. Apparently, it is simply not as much fun to hate the Yankees, or the system that enables their despised supremacy, if they fail to assume the role of pillaging horde on an annual basis. Most message boards featured a variety of quick-hitting digs regarding the Yankees' recent woes, substituting a tone of mocking superiority for the usual jealousy-soaked hatred. Resisting such taunts in favor of a more sober analysis, Tampa Bay Rays fan Upncoming offered one of the more thoughtful explanations of this recent development:

> I can't think of the last free agent that the Yanks overpaid for that hasn't burned them. But still, having such a history, especially recent history, of financial irresponsibility and never seeing them get hurt because of it really leaves a bad taste in a lot of people's mouths. Give $90 million to Carl Pavano and he barely ever pitches for us? Giambi getting $20 million a year for those three years when he was the twenty-fifth best first baseman in MLB? The left side of the infield making more than most teams? They print money, so it never comes back to bite them. It really eats at fans of teams who literally have to get every move exactly right or they're trading away players. It's a very uneven playing field. Fortunately, the Yankees' seven-year drought, combined with World Series wins from the Marlins and D-backs, proves that you can build a champ without buying it. So there's hope to do it right.[66]

Complementing this inverse correlation between Yankee hatred and Yankee losses is the rise of an alternate object of fan hatred: the Boston Red Sox. While hatred borne of regional rivalries trumps Yankee hatred for some fans (e.g., White Sox v. Cubs, Angels v. A's), hatred of the Red Sox has certainly become a growth industry in the 21st century. Pirates fan 21sthebest offers this representative sample of recently minted Red Sox hatred:

> I hate the Red Sox far more than I hate the Yankees. Actually, I don't even hate the Yankees. The Red Sox are as much a part of the problem as the Yankees are. And [Red Sox co-owner Larry] Lucchino referring to the Yankees as the evil empire was a joke. He's not better than Steinbrenner.[67]

But some fans, like Phillies supporter Ben29, see the Red Sox as victims of circumstance who are merely following in the Yankees' footsteps:

> I hate the Yankees. Well, basically because they ruined baseball with the ridiculous contracts they give to players. They are the reason small market teams can't compete. They are the reason players do not stay with one team

for their career. And don't tell me Boston does it also. Because Boston and other teams would not if it were not for those rotten Yankees driving up player prices.[68]

Still others, like Reds fan TS20, see both Red Sox hatred and Yankee hatred as more of an intramural event:

> The real hate exists in Boston and New York, with fans hating each other's teams. The rest of us take pleasure when the money teams lose, but that is the extent of it.[69]

Of course, it has taken a good deal of time and effort for fans to refine the tradition of Yankee hatred. Perhaps since it is still in its infancy, some Red Sox hatred suffers from an impulsive excess, a tendency exemplified beautifully by the following tale told by San Diego Padres fan Bossk:

> I had a flight to San Jose the day after last year's series with the Red Sox and the check-in lines were backed-up to the door with people in Boston gear. It took me forever to check in my luggage and I barely made my flight. Anyway, when I arrived at my destination, I apparently checked-in my luggage too late in San Diego and had to wait two hours in the San Jose airport for it to arrive on another flight. I pretty much blame Boston fans for all my misfortunes. Except for maybe my herpes. I think she was a Dodgers fan.[70]

It's not surprising that the Red Sox should become a secondary focus for some of the hatred previously reserved for the Yankees. They're wealthy, recently successful, and enjoy that East Coast media bias which is at the heart of so much of that Yankee hatred. But if we can judge from the comments offered here, it's not as if the Red Sox provide a purer iconic focus for fan resentment. Just as in the more time-honored phenomenon of Yankee hatred, a palpable ambivalence is woven into this new antipathy. It's as if the fans are still not quite sure what to hate. Perhaps it is possible that hatred of Red Sox Nation could one day eclipse Yankee hatred as a focus for fan frustrations. But it would be unwise to hold our collective breath on that one.

So, what remains of the notion that Yankee hatred is all about this diabolical system of the evil empire and the institution of Major League Baseball that enables it? Well, there's not a lot of love lost on that current personification of evil, Yankees' owner George Steinbrenner. But scratch the surface of all that venom directed his way and you'll find a good measure of respect alongside the hatred. At once, fans seem both resentful and admiring of his status as a fabulously wealthy member of a powerful elite, simultaneously railing against his obnoxious personality and acknowledging that those very character traits have contributed significantly to an enviable winning tradition. Fans don't necessarily want to have a beer with such a nasty guy, yet they stand in awe of what such nastiness can achieve. Then there's the matter of all those championships that all that wealth has supposedly purchased. While it's difficult for fans that have trouble scraping together the cash needed to rent one of the cheap seats to accept the influence of all that Yankee money, it seems almost equally difficult for them to view the use of that money by an autonomous entity as clearly inappropriate. After all, it is *their* money. What right does anyone else have to tell them how to spend it? For many fans, to do so would be contrary to the American way, a belief that likewise pertains to the issue of big-market teams having an advantage over small-market teams. Maybe big markets get big for a reason, and maybe they deserve the bigger share of the pie that Major League Baseball is so unwilling to deny them. But an unconditional embrace of such big-city favoritism certainly rubs fans in Cleveland and Kansas City the wrong way. While trying to fix that economic disparity through the imposition of some sort of salary cap seems consistent with the American virtue of equality, it also chafes against even the most proletarian fan's suspicion of socialism, welfare, and free lunches of all kinds. Then there's that problem of East Coast media bias, which might actually solve itself to some degree if fans across the country would simply turn off the television.

Across this spectrum of complaints about the system, it seems that most fanbases struggle with negotiating the conflicting values of individual freedom versus institutional stability, privileged wealth versus dignified privation, and survival of the fittest versus the rule-bound equality of a level playing field. Perhaps this ambivalence is a product of having to deal with elements of a system that are simply beyond the ken of those fans that must thrive in its wake, a predicament not unlike trying to deal with realities determined on Wall Street by using life experience acquired on Main Street. Indeed, factors like markets, finance, media, and other elements of Major League Baseball's infrastructure are relentlessly thing-like. Even George Steinbrenner ends up getting treated more like an object than a real human being, his flesh-and-blood personhood being secondary in the minds of many fans to his function within the system. Maybe the system is just too inanimate to inspire a passionate hatred that is beyond question. Maybe that requires something a little closer to home, something more organic, something carbon-based. Like that annoying Yankee fan in the seat next to you.

Chapter 4

IT'S ABOUT THE FANS

In the spring of 1990, I was working as a temporary, untenured member of the faculty on which I now serve as a fully promoted and tenured professor. In terms of the daily routine, the difference between these two positions is barely noticeable. In each case, one goes to work, teaches classes, attends meetings, grades papers, and tries to generate a program of scholarship that demonstrates an expertise capable of ensuring future employment. Perhaps the biggest difference could be best described in terms of security; not just the job security that comes with tenure and results in few worries of a pink slip showing up on your desk any given Monday morning, but also the collegial security that comes from acceptance by one's peers as an intellectually and culturally worthy member of the academy. Back in my temporary, untenured days, I was always on the lookout for opportunities to cultivate that sort of acceptance. I chose to pass on some of them, especially when it seemed that my efforts were likely to result in an embarrassing faux pas, exposing me as the unsophisticated Philistine I always feared I was. But when one of my colleagues invited me to a party celebrating the completion of his doctoral degree, I saw it as a fairly safe suck-up opportunity. Everyone from work would be there, even some of our students. So, that uncomfortable feeling of being in a room with no one familiar to talk to would not be a concern. Also, it was a party, where drinks would be served, and where some would be served too many. So, there was a good chance that I would not be the only person likely to do something stupid during the course of the evening. Add to this the fact that not going would clearly be a snub to a guy who had been nothing but helpful and friendly to me, and the decision to go became a real no-brainer. The event was being hosted by a good friend of his who, by virtue of a combination of rent control and trust fund checks, lived in an apartment in midtown Manhattan that was spacious enough to accommodate the festivities. So, I began the 75-mile drive to New York City with a relatively carefree attitude, my main concern being the location of an appropriate parking space.

I had a great time that evening for several reasons, not the least of which was meeting a young woman who found me inoffensive enough to approach and actually speak to me. Being free, single, and suitably immature at the time, I jumped at the chance to reciprocate her attention, and by the end of the evening, I had a phone number prefaced by a New York City area code scribbled on a matchbook in my shirt pocket. Driving back to Pennsylvania that night, I felt as if I had met the city on its own terms and came away victorious, in possession of a trophy that would serve as my return ticket to even greater adventures in urban excitement. After allowing an appropriate period of time to pass in order to avoid the appearance of being pathetically anxious, I dialed the number with the intent of making a date. We agreed to make our second meeting a relatively casual and unstructured day in New York, during which we would just go with the flow and get to know one another better. Of course, it's that part about getting to know one another better where it all goes to hell in a handbasket. Sure, things started out just fine; we scored a couple tickets for Free Shakespeare in the Park, got caught in the rain, bought matching sweatshirts to replace our soaked clothes, took some photos, and had some laughs. Then, we got to know one another better. "Your boyfriend got busted for what?" "How long is his jail sentence?" "You really think you can afford this apartment working as a sign language interpreter for music videos?" It's not that any of this would completely disqualify her as a fine and upstanding human being worthy of my time and attention. But of all the weird variables and mixed messages I received that day, there's one thing that stands out as the deal-breaker.

While passing one of the many markets openly displaying its produce on the sidewalk to potential customers, we decided to buy a couple of peaches to eat while strolling back to her place. Not wanting to appear displeased with a peach more memorable for its exorbitant price than its juice content, I did battle with this urban excuse for fresh fruit until I reached the pit. Relieved that I had finished without requiring a napkin or another change of clothes, I placed the peach pit in a sidewalk planter filled with old soil and a tree sapling struggling for life amid the exhaust fumes. Then, it happened: "Hey, that's a planter, not a trash can! Don't throw your garbage in there!" As she spoke these words, I was initially shocked by her angry tone. Then, I was amazed by her stupidity. Call me a country bumpkin if you must, but we're talking about a biodegradable peach pit being placed in a container full of earth, and she's looking at me like I'm the captain of the *Exxon Valdez*. My *garbage*? Back in the Midwest of my childhood, we called this *composting*, a return of nature's remnants to their natural home. Sorry, lady, but that's a good thing! Who knows, that peach pit might even attempt to take root and grow in this horrific concrete nightmare you choose to call home. For the remainder of that long and uncomfortably quiet walk to her apartment, I could only wonder how being raised in New York City, with all the educational and cultural advantages that implies, could result in a person so oblivious to the difference between the gracefully interwoven products of the natural world and the industrial-age flotsam she wraps up in plastic bags before shipping them off to a landfill in what is now my backyard in Pennsylvania. Man, there's just something about these New Yorkers.

As time passed, I began to think that maybe it was just something about her. After all, it's not wise to assume that all New Yorkers are that clueless about things that seem so obvious to folks like me. Then, the people next door moved in. Nice folks, don't get me wrong. Like many families that have moved to the Pocono Mountains during the last couple of decades, they were New Yorkers in search of open space, better schools, and lower taxes. The Poconos might represent the last opportunity for a New Yorker to find these things; residential areas in New Jersey, Connecticut, and Long Island within a reasonable commuting distance from Manhattan have been fully developed for quite some time, and the urban issues motivating the exodus from the city are often replicated in these places for all but the most affluent. So, the human face of the city now finds itself eyeball-to-eyeball with unshaven dudes in blaze-orange headgear carrying deer rifles and looking to pierce Bambi's flesh right behind the shoulder. The results of this bizarre social experiment in urban-rural coexistence can be amusing at times. But more often, it seems to generate a sort of low-grade mutual annoyance. As a member of the rural team, I can only imagine and try to appreciate the true nature of the urbanite's vexation. But I can almost hear the collective groan of the locals when a newly transplanted New Yorker, convinced that he's in the wilderness because he can't find a slice of pizza for sale within walking distance of his front door, decides that this odd condition of darkness that occurs after sundown is simply untenable and proceeds to install exterior lighting that would dwarf the candlepower produced by any of the nation's major airports. An individualized version of this communal displeasure can undoubtedly be heard inside every local's car when brakes must be applied in order to avoid hitting the newly arrived city kids playing football in the street, oblivious to the fact that the vacant half-acre of lawn in front of their house might provide a better venue. But hey, what's the big deal? We're in the wilderness here! Fugged-aboudit! Sure, some New Yorkers who make this move to the Poconos do so more gracefully, having vacationed in the area during the summers and weekends of their youth. But even that level of familiarity is not enough to overcome the cultural divide in the eyes of long-time local residents, some of whom still proudly display bumper stickers that read, "If they call it tourist season, why can't I shoot them?"

But anyway, back to those nice folks next door. Seizing the opportunity to buy an undeveloped piece of land, they eagerly arranged for the construction of a massive residence capable of housing a very extended family: the elderly matriarch of the clan, her retired minister husband, their thirtyish schoolteacher daughter, her husband with a job in the city, their infant son, a few nieces and nephews in dire need of escape from the New York City public schools, and perhaps a few others I'm not aware of. While the house was under construction, either grandma or daughter would periodically phone us from their home in the Bronx—within view of their beloved Yankee Stadium—to get updates on their project in the Poconos. Soon, moving day arrived, and their dream of rural simplicity became a reality. Well, at least they moved into the house. How dreamlike their lives became is a judgment call, to say the least. Shortly after their move, the daughter, her husband, and their child decided to get a place just north of the city, finding the strain of the daily commute to be a bit too cumbersome. I'm not really sure if grandpa ever made the move, as I was never able to make a confirmed sighting of him. I think the nieces and nephews toughed it out until the end of the school year. Eventually, it was just grandma, alone in the biggest house on the street. One day, she phoned, ostensibly to just say hello, but the conversation quickly turned to what was clearly a more urgent matter as she asked, "When do the buses run by here?" Uhh, *buses*? Sorry, but most of the buses in this town are the ones that take the commuters to and from Manhattan every day, and those buses sure don't stop anywhere near our street. The realization quickly sank in. The nice old lady next door, like many native New Yorkers, had never owned a car, had never driven a car, and had always been completely reliant upon public transportation for any travel beyond her front door. The next few weeks were graced with the sight of the guy from the Sears Driving School showing up next door, trying in vain to convert this unfortunate woman into an operator of motor vehicles. After exhausting that hopeless option, a portion of the house was rented to some folks who not only kept a watchful eye on this stranger in a strange land, but whose rent checks probably enabled the avoidance of a mortgage foreclosure. These days, the whole house is a rental, occupied by a stream of college students, itinerant workers, and unshaven dudes in blaze-orange headgear carrying deer rifles.

It's a sad tale, really. Like I said, they really were nice folks. But they were New Yorkers, and there's just something about these New Yorkers. That all this hardship could result from a New Yorker's naive assumption that basic human needs, like transportation, are somehow magically addressed by any number of benevolent bureaucratic agencies is simply tragic. In fact, it's infuriating, though not quite as infuriating as what's-her-name referring to my peach pit as garbage. In either case, we have good evidence that these New Yorkers are just different from the rest of Americans in some very elemental ways, and, by extension, so are the members of that subspecies of New Yorkers who call themselves Yankee fans.

To be honest, my own experience with Yankee fans has not been all that dreadful. As an expatriate Indians fan living a full day's drive from Cleveland and less than 90 minutes from Yankee Stadium, I have found myself sitting in the House That Ruth Built on a few occasions when the Tribe was in town and I had the day free. The first of these visits was the most memorable, as it was 1999, and the Indians were experiencing a rare period of success during which they stood as a major threat to Yankee hegemony. Emboldened by their prowess on the field, I chose to enter enemy territory in full Tribe regalia, fearing no Yankee fan. As it turned out, there was really nothing to fear in the Bronx that day; some good-natured pregame argument in the bar across the street, no awkward confrontations in the less public confines of the stadium men's room, and no concessionaire-supplied projectiles hurled my way for an entire nine innings. I even managed to summon up the requisite goose bumps as I approached the edifice for the first time. As the evening wore on, this pleasant spectator experience almost had me regretting the revulsion that would always arise whenever I thought of the Yankees and their fans. Then, as Manny Ramirez was finishing his warm-up tosses in the outfield before the bottom of one of the game's late innings, he jogged over to the right-field stands and handed the baseball to a little boy sporting head-to-toe Yankee merchandise. For a moment, I wondered what motivated Manny to engage in this Norman Rockwell moment; he did grow up in New York and might be doing this as some sort of hometown kindness, or perhaps he realized that he was just a season and a half away from hitting the free agent market and was engaging in a little positive image building. Then, remembering that this was Manny Ramirez and that only a fool would attempt to discern any logic behind any of his behaviors, my attention was redirected toward that little boy, who sat expressionless as he calmly took possession of the ball without so much as uttering a word. As I sat calculating just how many of my limbs I would have gladly sacrificed in order to be personally presented with a souvenir baseball by a real Major Leaguer when I was this kid's age, I could arrive at only one explanation for his nonchalance: the kid's a

Yankee fan and, even at a very young age, they think they deserve this kind of treatment. It was probably all the kid could do to resist asking Ramirez for his glove, too. As evidence of the acorn not falling far from the oak, the man I assumed to be the kid's father just sat there next to him, every bit as indifferent to this extraordinary event as was his young charge. I mean, he didn't even gently prod the little twerp to offer a thank you! This would never happen in Cleveland, I thought, or in any other Major League town outside of New York. Oh yeah, there really *is* something about these New Yorkers.

So, what exactly is it? For lack of a better term, let's just call it attitude. While there are probably as many stories illustrating that attitude as there are people who are not New Yorkers, maybe the phenomenon is best encapsulated by Saul Steinberg, illustrator and cartoonist for *The New Yorker* from 1942 until his death in 1999, who created *A View of the World from Ninth Avenue* for the cover of the March 29, 1976, issue of the magazine. Serving as a formulaic template for several subsequent critiques of cultural myopia, the bottom half of Steinberg's original drawing featured an accurately detailed foreground of several blocks on Manhattan's West Side, bordered by the Hudson River. Beyond this precise depiction of New York real estate lies the remainder of the world; a neatly drawn rectangle representing the rest of the United States, the near edge of which is the thin brown strip of New Jersey, a few randomly chosen states and major cities sprinkled about, with Canada to the right, Mexico to the left, the Pacific Ocean in the distance, and the nondescript lumps of China, Russia, and Japan beyond. Of course, the eternal question here is one of perspective: Does Steinberg's drawing illustrate the way in which self-centered New Yorkers view the world beyond their city, or does it represent how the rest of us view the opinion New Yorkers have of themselves? But for those who hate the New York Yankees and their fans, this rhetorical distinction certainly seems to be a silly one. You bet that's the way New Yorkers view the world, and all those baseball fans west of the Hudson River are on to them, and what's generally true for New Yorkers has got to be true for all those Yankee fans, right?

Well, truth be told, ambivalent attitudes about New York attitude abound. A survey of employees and entrepreneurs across the country was recently conducted in order to determine America's favorite and least-favorite cities in which to live and work. Presented with the scenario of being offered a dream job that required geographical relocation, respondents chose New York City as *both* their favorite and least-favorite destination.[1] While this strange dichotomy can be interpreted in a number of ways, it seems to stand as an acknowledgement of the privileged status New Yorkers hold in the social hierarchy of American culture. After all, who wouldn't relish enjoying the rewards of living in a place where one feels justified in defining the world as it appears from the balcony of their condo on Ninth Avenue? Of course, raising their collective hand in response to this question are all those who must remain on the other side of the Hudson River, and therein lies the rub. Not everyone will be offered that dream job in New York City, so anyone who accepts such an offer only serves to reinforce the exceptionalism at the heart of all that New York attitude. It's this same exceptionalism in Yankee fans that makes other baseball fans feel the way the rest of the world must feel about Americans: simultaneously drawn to, and repelled by, the confidence and swagger it generates. Exceptionalism doesn't mix well with those values of democracy and equality so cherished in the mythology of the American heartland; values which, like a lifelong allegiance to one's hometown team, can't simply be expunged from a person's character because they're offered a sweet gig in the city. Speaking of which, who, other than those imbued with New York attitude, would ever refer to their city as "*the* city?" Only those with the temerity to refer to a peach pit as garbage, if you ask me!

Ambivalent feelings about the attitude exhibited by Yankee fans is occasionally expressed by fans posting on the message boards, and Pirates fan Doc hamp even attempts a rational understanding of it in his response to a fellow fan's complaint about New York exceptionalism:

> I think it's your prerogative to build up a good hatred for a team. We've all probably done that whether that regards the Phillies, Mets, Reds, Browns, Bengals, Flyers, Rangers, etc. That sort of thing makes sports fun, as long as the hating fan doesn't get carried away at a park and does something regrettable. But you asked in your post why New York should be the center of the baseball universe. To be honest, they should. Baseball, as we know it today, was born there and it was their style of game that spread to the rest of the country just before and then after the Civil War. I think New Yorkers are justifiably proud of that and, if I were from New York, I'd feel the same way.[2]

Of course, Yankee haters would be quick to suggest to Doc hamp that he should *not* feel the same way as proud Yankee fans because he is *not* from New York. Since it's probably safe to assume he hasn't been offered one of those dream jobs requiring relocation to the Big Apple, perhaps his attempt to walk a mile in a Yankee fan's shoes will remain purely hypothetical.

Far more common among baseball fans are statements acknowledging what is seen as a painfully obvious line of division between the Yankee faithful and the rest of baseball fandom; between New Yorkers and the rest of America. Diamondbacks fan SarBear sums it up succinctly:

> It's not just the team, the Yankees. It's their fans, too. I've never come across a more egotistical, obnoxious lot of people. New Yorkers in general just annoy me.[3]

DeronJ, a fan of the Cincinnati Reds, echoes this sentiment, though a bit more sarcastically:

> Twenty million arrogant New Yorkers blowing about a franchise that's had the pick of the talent litter for the last 100 years. What's to like?[4]

In his explanation of Yankee hatred, Detroit Tigers fan Kidoist takes a swipe at the supposed sophistication assumed to be a natural byproduct of living in New York City:

> I think much of the hatred is due to the vulgar fans. Their arrogance and x-rated mouthiness would be acceptable if they had anything to do with their team's performance. But they don't, except for purchasing tickets, eating ball park hotdogs, and spilling their beer on their shirts.[5]

This environment of virulent Yankee hatred is occasionally graced with a plea for moderation and balance as the foundation for the development of a healthy fanbase. A Twins fan posting to the Diamondbacks message boards, Bizz12, in no way excuses the widely acknowledged attitude problem of Yankee fans, but he does interpret that attitude as a consequence of Yankee fans being spoiled by an excess of success:

> Granted, every ball club has some unruly fans, but it's hard for me to have a mentality like Yankees fans do. Going into every season I hope that, just once, the Yankees would either miss the playoffs or have a losing season . . . Sure, I would love to be a fan of a team that has high expectations every year and wins a lot of games. But sometimes too much winning can be a bad thing, as evidenced on these very boards. If more fans could be classy about it, then maybe I'd have a different perspective on this. But it's like they're poisoned by it. I choose to be a Twins fan because it's the first MLB team I've followed since age 12. I stand by them through the good and the bad. I have enough of both so I can truly appreciate the game. It's like plants, gardens, grass & flowers. They all need the sun, but too much sun can be damaging. They also need the rain, and too much rain can also be damaging. They need a healthy balance of both to grow. And while I hope the Twins & D-Backs win every year and play each other in the World Series, realistically that's unlikely. I think too much winning and too much losing can really poison

a team's fan base. And the two teams I would quickly point at in this case would be the Yankees and the Royals. Talk about two extremes. What I really think it comes down to regarding the hatred for the Yankees is a lot of fans wish their favorite team could be in a position like the Yankees, who can pretty much afford anybody and be a perennial winner. Yankees fans don't know the reality of what the rest of us fans go through, and if they did it would slap them a lot harder than it would the rest of us. I don't think they can truly, and I mean truly, appreciate winning until they get the taste of losing. And I'm not just talking about making the playoffs and getting an early exit.[6]

It's almost as if Bizz12 is claiming that Yankee fans are the victims here; that they are actually denied something that builds the character of fans that follow less successful teams. But it seems that whenever Yankee haters are presented such an opportunity to develop an empathic response to Yankee fan attitude, a Yankee fan like Elek5 has to go and open his big mouth:

Are you serious with this topic? Most people hate the Yankees? Are you trying to act dumb or is it just natural? The largest fan base in baseball and you say most people hate them? Very odd assumption . . . Anyone who "hates" the Yankees is just a sore loser and jealous. Plain and simple.[7]

Okay, so a Yankees fan engages in some tough talk in defense of his team. While Yankee haters might not appreciate Elek5's tone, many can appreciate his passion. But when Yankeesvictory, a Yankees fan monitoring the Yankee hatred thread on the Colorado Rockies Message Boards, musters up a provisional allegiance to the Rockies based on their 2007 World Series appearance against the Red Sox and then threatens to withhold it if his false love is not authentically reciprocated, who could blame a Yankee hater for rekindling their rancor:

I fiercely supported you people in the World Series. I hoped against hope that you would pull off an upset. I held onto that hope until the very last out. It didn't matter that it was the ninth inning of Game Four and [Red Sox closer Jonathan] Papelbon was on the mound. I still rooted for you guys until the bitter end. And this is how you repay me? This is not good for our relationship.[8]

Now, *that's* attitude.

Still, we should consider the possibility that this attitude problem is not necessarily generated by any Yankee fan's sheer force of will in pursuit of the goal of being obnoxious. Indeed, there may be some very sound, logical reasons to assume that Yankee fan attitude is a product of environmental nurture rather than individual nature. For instance, to say that New York City is the center of Western civilization would not be an indefensible statement. As a major hub of commerce and culture, New York City affords its residents an array of entertainment options unparalleled by just about any other city with a Major League ball club. Though it never occurred to me while growing up an Indians fan in Greater Cleveland, a reasonable explanation of why we are such a dedicated lot may stem from the fact that, during the bulk of the baseball season, the Tribe is the only show in town. Conversely, in addition to being spoiled by an incredible diversity of shows in town on a daily basis, New Yorkers even have the option of choosing between two Major League ball clubs. Sure, the same can be said for a few other locales in Major League Baseball, but the dynamic of intramural fandom in these places is just not the same. Chicago is blessed with a mutual loathing between fans of the Cubs and White Sox dating so far back that no one seems to remember where it all started, but everyone in the Windy City seems to understand it as a signifier of the never-ending class conflict between the North Side and South Side; effete snobs who shower in order to go to the office and honest laborers who must do so after a hard day's work. California's Bay Area, home to two somewhat recently transplanted franchises in the A's and Giants, has developed two fanbases that seem too preoccupied with small-market anxiety to develop a respectable level of mutual disgust. Fans in Southern California seem to have settled into a comfortable culture war played out between the caricatured fanbases of the Angels and Dodgers; take your pick of two stadiums filled to capacity with either numbingly bland suburbanites or a variety of street gangs strapped for battle. Though the particulars vary, these three multi-team markets seem to have developed multi-fanbase dynamics characterized by a rough equality, in which each fanbase gives as good as it gets. Not so in New York, where the relationship between Yankees fans and Mets fans is anything but a two-way street.

Mets fans seem to be keeping up their end of the fan rivalry bargain, as evidenced by this narrative posted to the Mets message boards by AdRock18:

> I'm 33 and I've hated this team forever. I remember being in a Brooklyn bowling alley packed with Yankee fans when [the Seattle Mariners'] Edgar Martinez beat them in October of '95. I started celebrating wildly, and then all of the Yankee fans started giving me really mean glares. It was time to leave. Today, I hate them even more, due to the fans. The Yankees have become a parody, a joke. In my gym, I see tons of these young, tanned, tattooed and steroided kids all walking around with their Yankee hats on their heads, which are sitting on top of their shoulders; no necks, of course. Meanwhile, these kids couldn't tell you who [former Yankees] Greg Nettles or Oscar Gamble were. I think that 99.7% of these tattooed juiceheads you

see on the city streets are "Yankee" fans. God, I wish all of these kids would get hit by a bus.[9]

Theroostah, a Red Sox fan who grew up in New York as a non-Yankee fan, continues to harbor his own Yankee hatred, indicating that localized Yankee hatred may even extend beyond Mets fans to supporters of any New York team not named the Yankees:

It isn't the players that are hated but rather the Yankee organization and their obnoxious fans. I grew up a Brooklyn Dodger fan and all we ever heard from Yankee fans was how great Babe Ruth and Lou Gerhig were, and how great [Joe] DiMaggio was. When Mickey Mantle came along, all you ever heard was how great he was; even better than Willie Mays (which, of course, was absurd). Every time Mantle hit a home run, the Yankee press agents would pull out a tape measure. Every time the Yanks won, their fans would gloat and say how great Casey Stengel was as a manager. And if the Pinstripes lost, their fans would remind you of their past glories. Now the tradition of hating the Yankees has spread to Mets fans as well. It's something in the psyche of Yankee fans that automatically makes them insufferable boors. When your team is really good (as are the Red Sox right now) you don't have to brag about it. It's enough just to know they are. But not for Yankee fans.[10]

A small number of others, like Mets fan Fargol, adopt a more accommodating stance borne of the opportunity to shift allegiances between two local teams and the need to justify that shift:

I've got nothing against them. I was a Yankee fan first, back in the very early 60s, then migrated to the Mets camp in the mid-60s. I used to root for them a lot more than I do now. Not sure why; I can't really get into many of the current players. I like Jeter, Posada, and Mariano, but none of the other guys do much for me. I loved the old-time players like [Chris] Chambliss, [Thurman] Munson, etc. But, for the last few years, I've been very passive about them. But, I don't hate the organization, or the fans. Yes, there are arrogant, obnoxious Yankee fans, but the Mets fanbase has them, too.[11]

Fargol's attempted compassion notwithstanding, it's fair to say that most Mets fans (and, perhaps, some old Brooklyn Dodgers fans) exhibit a healthy strain of Yankee hatred roughly equivalent to that found in the other fanbases of Major League Baseball.

As for Yankees fans and their perception of the Mets, it's clearly a different story. When a comment from a Yankees fan appears on a message board, any mention of their cross-town rival often comes across as an afterthought. Our old friend, Elek5, offers a cryptic example of this tendency when he claims not to "hate any team. Well, except the Mets, but that doesn't count. (-:"[12] Exactly *why* wouldn't that hatred count? Maybe it's a desire not to speak ill of any New York institution, even if it competes with his beloved Yankees for the affection of New Yorkers, which causes him to discount any Mets hatred he may feel. But the smiley-face emoticon at the end of his statement seems to betray another interpretation: this guy thinks the *Mets* don't count; that they are less a threat worth hating than they are something deserving of mockery and ridicule. Recalling his response to a White Sox fan's query regarding hatred between fans of the Yankees and Mets, Joe Queenan offers an answer that seems to support this view:

> I felt it was safe to say that Mets fans hated Yankee fans with a pathological ferocity not unlike what the Palestinians feel for the Israelis, whereas Yankees fans merely viewed Mets fans as a nuisance. I qualified my reply by noting that in using the term *nuisance*, I was not referring to something dangerous, like famished rats or meningitis-bearing raccoons in the attic. In the eyes of Yankees fans, both the Mets and their adherents were more of a pathetic inconvenience, like lint or shih tzu hairs. Since many Yankee fans were occupants of the very lowest rungs of the New York social ladder, this derision was triply infuriating to the Mets faithful.[13]

While a few Mets fans like Fargol appear willing and able to thoughtfully deal with the opportunity to be a fickle fan with more than one choice, Yankee fans generally seem incapable of acknowledging that the Mets even constitute a *valid* choice. While Fargol was not the only Mets fan to claim a prior allegiance to the Yankees, not a single Yankees fan posting to any message board cited even a passing infatuation with the Mets as a feature of their personal fan history. It's as if Yankees fans are capable of elevating New York exceptionalism to a level that can even exclude fellow New Yorkers. True, both fanbases are full of New Yorkers, and as we established earlier in this chapter, there really is something about these New Yorkers. But there's something *else* about New Yorkers who happen to be Yankees fans. At this juncture, a truism seems to be in order: You can take a Yankees fan out of New York, but you can't take the New York out of a Yankees fan, and there's no shortage of Yankees fans outside of New York to serve as test subjects for this hypothesis.

While New York City is a big place, it is simply not big enough to contain all those New Yorkers. Having run out of room in their native land, a sizeable New York diaspora has developed, and within it lurk many Yankee fans. As I mentioned earlier, I live in the midst of a significant concentration of these evacuees in the Pocono Mountains of Pennsylvania, and I have struggled to adapt not only to their urban ways, but to their Yankee fandom, as well. Let's just say it has not been an entirely pleasant experience. Having already noted that my few experiences with Yankee fans in their natural habitat of Yankee Stadium have been reasonably cordial and noncombative, it's a whole different ballgame with these folks when they're off their home turf. When in the Bronx, it's almost as if Yankee fans make an extra effort to live down their reputation as repugnant jerks by being exceptionally hospitable in the presence of an outsider. But put them outside that comfort zone and their defensiveness about their fandom starts to resemble the behavior of a rabid badger cornered by animal control deputies. In the Poconos, most of those guys from animal control are wearing Phillies jerseys, and the number of displaced rabid badgers continues to grow, while it appears that animal control has instituted a hiring freeze. Now that a rough parity in numbers has been established in the area, it's becoming easier to make a fair comparison of those old, entrenched Phillies fans and the invading pinstriped horde. Let's cut to the chase: one group expects to win as if it is part of a birthright, and the other is simply hopeless. I'll allow the reader to figure out which is which. I know, the Phillies are fresh off a 2008 World Series victory. How could Phillies fans possibly be hopeless? Well, that's certainly a good question for which I don't have a good answer. Maybe it's in the water, or the gene pool, or some weird fan version of a tragically inexplicable cancer cluster. All I can tell you after living among the Phillies faithful for the past 20 years is that I've never encountered a more dismal, pessimistic bunch of fans in my life. While they seem as loyal as any other fanbase, their loyalty appears to be exclusively spent as dues that must be paid in order to reserve the right to endlessly complain about the Phillies before the season even starts. When former Cleveland Indian Jim Thome was considering whether to remain with my beloved Tribe or sign with the Phillies back in 2002, I briefly contemplated sending him a cautionary e-mail about the ghastly fan-player dynamic he was about to walk into should he choose to accept the Phillies' contract offer. In Cleveland, the man was a virtual baseball deity. So eager were Tribe fans to retain his services that there was serious talk of a contractual article ensuring the erection of a statue of him outside the entrance to what was then known as Jacobs Field. After a few years in Philadelphia, regardless of his performance on the field, he'd be lucky to escape with the majority of his internal organs intact. Of course, I never did send him that e-mail, so I really can't say I told him so. But Jim, considering the way things turned out, I really should have told you so. The vast attitudinal difference between these Phillies fans and Yankees fans is brought into graphic relief every spring in my own university classroom, as the talk turns to baseball during the minutes before class is called to order. Judging from a quick count of baseball caps in the room, these fanbases are rather equally represented. But any similarity ends there, as the Yankee faithful sit back with that smug grin on their faces, knowing that any weakness in their lineup that revealed itself during spring training would be remedied with piles of cash before the July trading deadline arrived. As for the Phillies fans, they're a little jazzed about the prospect of going to the ballpark on a sunny day and knocking back a few cold ones. But most of them have already developed their three-page list of reasons why the Phillies will finish in fourth place or lower. And this is in *April*! I could go on, but let's allow Green420, a Baltimore Orioles fan living in the Poconos, to sum up the situation:

> I hate the Stankees because I live in the Poconos. It is often referred to as the sixth borough of New York. Everybody around me is a New York-born Stankee fan. I can't go into public in an O's shirt without one of them making a smart remark like, "Did you lose a bet and have to wear that shirt?" Can't stand most of them.[14]

Eclipsing this invasion of the Poconos by Yankee fans in both size and vigor is the beachhead they have established in Florida. These Yankee fans, either old enough to retire there or wealthy enough to spend the winter there as "snowbirds," have created a qualitatively different dynamic than that found on the northern front, perhaps due to the fact that they are about 1,000 miles from home. Yes, these displaced rabid badgers are a long way from the den, and the resultant intensity of their defensiveness is amply reflected on the message boards of the two teams located in the Sunshine State. Perhaps the thing that most vexes the Yankee haters of Florida, and which rarely occurs in the Poconos, is the phenomenon of transplanted Yankee fans developing a secondary fandom for one of the local teams. To think that a Yankee fan would begin to follow the Phillies simply because she moves a couple of zip codes west is absurd. But a Yankee fan condescending to support either the Rays or the Marlins, all the while remaining a devoted Yankee fan, seems de rigueur following that move down south. At the close of his aforementioned defense of his cherished Yankees on the Florida Marlins Message Boards, Elek5 offers the following infuriating coda:

> So, I really think the "haters" are really a small minority of jealous, pseudo baseball fans. Oh, and I now like the Marlins since I moved to South Florida. Go Fish![15]

Not surprisingly, carpetbagger commentary like this elicits a good deal of angry reaction from homegrown fans, such as this salvo from Rays fan Upncoming:

> In years when they've been good recently and the Rays have been bad (which until this year was a given), Yankee fans would fill up the Trop

[Tampa's Tropicana Field] and they are just so in-your-face. They look New York, dress New York, talk New York, and act New York. I always ask if New York is so f'in' great, WHY ARE YOU ALL HERE? I have yet to get a response that is worthwhile. When the Yanks win in the Trop, they are all party and happy. If the Rays beat them, they immediately go to the "26 World Series" card. No matter the outcome, they are great and we suck.[16]

This issue of Yankee fans talking trash in other people's houses is hardly limited to Florida. Yankee fans don't actually have to assume a new mortgage and become your neighbor to end up sitting next to you at the ballpark. They've got attitude. They've got frequent flyer miles. And they're coming to a stadium near you. Just ask White Sox fan Chgophil what that's like:

What really kills the Yankees for me is the behavior of these fans when they visit other parks. Red Sox fans are loud and obnoxious, and they have become quite intolerable over the last four years, but all they really do is cheer for their team as if they were at Fenway. Yankee fans, conversely, taunt and curse at the home fans in their own park, insult the other team more than they cheer for their own, and speak with a self-righteousness in quotes like, "Being a Yankee fan, all I have to do is open a baseball almanac to shut anybody up." In the seasons that the White Sox miss the playoffs, my primary joy is rooting against the Yankees.[17]

So common were complaints like this in so many different message boards that one begins to suspect that not all of these Yankees fans in strange places are, or ever have been, New Yorkers. Honestly, how many frequent flyer miles could these Gothamites really rack up?

In his book about the college basketball rivalry between North Carolina and Duke, Will Blythe suggests that the respective cultural mindsets of the two schools is analogous to the difference between what he considers to be two kinds of Americans:

. . . those for whom the word "home" summons up an actual place that is wood-smoke fragrant with memory and desire, a place that one has no choice but to proudly claim, even if it's a falling-down dogtrot shack, the place to which the compass always points, the place one visits in nightly dreams, the place to which one aims always to return, no matter how far off course the ship might drift.

And then there are those citizens for whom home is a more provisional notion—the house or apartment in which one sleeps at night, as if American life were an exhausting tour of duty, and home, no matter how splendid, equaled a mere rest stop on the Interstate of Personal Advancement. I am

biased against this kind of nomadism, no matter how well upholstered the
vehicles. The loss of adhesion to a particular place seems ruinous, and those
without the first kind of home wander through our nation like the flesh eaters
from *Night of the Living Dead*.[18]

Judging from the fans' message board postings, there's a lot of those flesh
eaters out there wearing Yankees gear who have never been east of the
Hudson River. Variously referred to as *bandwagon* or *fair-weather* fans,
it appears that these folks inspire even greater animus than the likes of
Elek5, that New Yorker who moved to South Florida and became some
sort of a half-Yankees/half-Marlins fan hybrid. The following comment
from Poleymak, a Mets fan posting to the Atlanta Braves Message Boards,
provides an example of the typical complaint regarding the bandwagon
Yankees fan:

> I think I also don't like the bandwagon Yankees fans. There are many legiti-
> mate fans that have loved their team for years. But, there is also the share
> of fans who've only rooted for the Yankees since they started to win World
> Series'. Previously, they were fans of other teams.[19]

At least Elek5 had the decency to actually move to Florida before declaring
himself a Marlins fan, and no one could ever accuse the guy of dumping a
loser for a winner. Additionally, retaining some allegiance to the Yankees
in absentia does make him appear less fickle and rootless in his fandom
than those who would latch on to whatever team might be winning at the
moment. Schwender7, an Orioles fan, reflects the popular sentiment that
geographic proximity to a team's home city is a prerequisite for appropriate fandom:

> Not only are most New Yorkers Yankee fans, but you can see Yankees hats
> in every city across the country. These are the bandwagon fans who follow
> the Yankees for no other reason than a long history of winning, but have no
> ties to the city or sport otherwise.[20]

Poleymak and Schwender7 invoke what seem to be the twin pillars of
complaint when it comes to the bandwagon or fair-weather Yankees fan:
arriving at the victory party too late, and arriving from some place other
than New York City. Angels fan Daygloman2 melds these two complaints
nicely, slamming the Johnny-come-lately fans while granting an easement
to the hometown faithful:

> Their transplanted fans have made me a hater! Although the fans at Yankee
> Stadium seemed pretty cool to me, except for one person who was a jerk

(I was in full-on Halos gear). But I, being from hostile So Cal, put a stop to his sarcastic mouth! The braggarts have made me this way, people claiming rights to championships they weren't around to celebrate! Don't say twenty-six rings, say four rings, bandwagoners![21]

Of course, the phenomenon of bandwagon or fair-weather fandom extends beyond those who claim an illegitimate connection to Yankee pinstripes. I personally know more than a few Miami Dolphins fans, all of whom have two things in common: their interest in following professional sports developed during the Dolphins' winning heyday of the 1970s, and none of them living anywhere near Miami. This same bandwagon recipe applies to many Dallas Cowboys fans minted in the 1980s, fans of the Chicago Bulls' dynasty of the 1990s, and several waves of Los Angeles Lakers bandwagoners, from Kareem to Kobe. It's not as if this disorder only afflicts spectators. Cleveland Cavaliers basketball star LeBron James endured a veritable tsunami of criticism when he showed up at Jacobs Field for a playoff game pitting the Indians against the Yankees in October of 2007 in a Yankees cap. James, who grew up in Akron, a mere 40 miles from Cleveland, plies his trade directly across the street from the Indians' ballpark, cheered on by members of the very fanbase he was seated with that evening. After several innings of rancorous reaction from those fans inspired him to leave the stands early, James calmly explained to an interviewer that he grew up a Yankees fan and felt obliged to support them, but was rooting for the Indians as individuals.[22] Now, it's touching that James supports the individuals inside those Tribe uniforms, and it's not like he became a Yankees fan last week. But fans need to feel that their sports heroes are like them in important, elemental ways; that they are fiercely loyal to the hometown and all of its institutions, not just to the guys who are currently employed by those institutions. Sorry, LeBron, but in the eyes of the average fan, that was traitorous behavior. Oh, by the way, his favorite football team? Why, it's the Dallas Cowboys, who had a string of Super Bowl appearances in the 1990s, when a young LeBron James was busy refining his fan preferences; how very, very bandwagon, LeBron. Ultimately, the bandwagon sports fan phenomenon seems largely motivated by the same impulse that results in many of my students seeking to relocate to Florida after graduation: they went there for a Disney World vacation when they were kids, had a blast, have held on to idealized memories of the experience ever since, and think they can recreate it as adults by moving there and working a 60-hour week. Who wouldn't choose a triumphant fantasy over the harsh reality of losing? Still, for every bandwagon fan who succumbs to the easy joys of borrowed victory, there are probably several others around them who have to endure the gloating. Nhraysfan, a Tampa Bay Rays supporter, cites this as the genesis of his own Yankee hatred:

> My hate for the Yankees was developed because I grew up living next door to the world's most obnoxious teenage Yankees fan. The year was 1970. This kid was such a BS shoveler even I (at 7 years old) could see through him. All summer long it was "Yankees are great, Yankees are great, Bobby Murcer is the best centerfielder ever, Thurman Munson is a god, etc., etc. By August, when I saw this kid coming towards me, I'd literally run inside and hide like he was the neighborhood bully.[23]

Now, I'm just assuming that this is not a New York story, and that this teenage Yankees fan was not a New Yorker and, therefore, a bandwagon Yankees fan. Otherwise, unless they were die-hard Mets fans, it's difficult to see why *both* of them weren't cheering on Murcer, Munson, and the rest of their home team. After all, that's what real, hometown fans are supposed to do.

As frequently cited as hometown loyalty is by fans in need of a litmus test for proper fandom, evidence does exist that its importance may lag behind other factors. In a study in which college students were asked the reason why they began to support, and continued to support, their favorite sports team, local team loyalty tied with peer influence as only the third-most prominent reason, behind the team loyalty of parents and the talent of the team's players. The team's success was an even less important factor in initial team identification, though it was the primary reason for maintaining that fandom over time.[24] However, a subsequent study revealed that fans of geographically distant teams displayed higher levels of support for more successful teams, leading to the conclusion that a winning record is a more important factor for fans that have moved away from their hometown than it is for those who remain local.[25] In other words, as social and geographical mobility become more prominent features of American life, it seems as if loyalty forged at a young age to one's hometown team is becoming a less important factor in the life of sports fans. Or, to put it bluntly, we may now have to consider bandwagon fandom to be a growth industry. Perhaps traditionalists will now have to adjust to a world where legitimate fandom can be achieved simply by following teams that happen to play nearest to one's residence of the moment, as opposed to expecting cradle-to-grave hometown loyalty. Referring to contemporary sport fanbases as "neo-tribes," sport sociologist Garry Crawford argues that these groupings are best viewed as *imagined* communities, whose authenticity is increasingly defined not by physical locality, but through the use and ownership of the appropriate media and consumer goods.[26] This conception of fandom as an exercise in shopping for commodities, rather than commitment to place, is often derided by fans that claim bandwagoners often support the Yankees simply because it is in vogue to do so:

> I actually have a lot of good friends that are Yankees fans. And yes, they can be obnoxious at times. But I bet I could name more current and past Yankees than they can put together. They root for them because it's fashionable.[27]

Judging from this statement by Pirates fan Goober21, it appears that some fans feel that owning that pinstriped jersey is no substitute for knowledge of the game and its players. But insisting upon a high degree of knowledge as a prerequisite for fandom is, frankly, bad for business. Sandvoss recognizes this reality in his assessment of the international appeal of sport "super clubs," like the Yankees and soccer's Manchester United, which he claims are marketed in an intentionally ambiguous manner in order to encourage the greatest number of fans to construct any number of personalized versions of fandom.[28] This consumer-friendly strategy for building the largest and, perhaps, shallowest fanbase possible not only ensures massive sales figures for official team merchandise, but also enables the misidentification of mere consumption as dedicated fandom:

> Most baseball fans LOVE the Yankees. The ones that don't are jealous of the Yankee success. You can go most anywhere, not only in the USA but worldwide, and you will see people wearing that NY logo on hats and shirts . . . Go to a professional game in ANY city and I'll guarantee you someone in the stands is wearing something with a Yankee logo. Go to the street markets of Asia and they sell Yankee caps . . . People LOVE the Yanks.[29]

For Seattle Mariners fan Enjoybb, it seems that the undying love of a genuine fan resides under every Yankees cap on earth. But, judging from fans' message board postings, this view is certainly a minority position. Far more typical is this assessment offered by Washington Nationals fan Natsfan11:

> As for the fans, a lot of people just act like they're Yankees fans, because you can find Yankees stuff pretty much in any baseball city. Some of the people who are "fans" really aren't. As for real Yankees fans, I wouldn't know. Never have been to a Yankees game while in New York.[30]

Queenan has coined his own synonym for the bandwagon or fair-weather fan: the *mainstream front-running fan*. In defining this sort of fan as an individual who consistently roots for a certain team only when they are winning, he is not necessarily talking about fans of any particular team. But since the Yankees do an awful lot of winning, and their fans seem to have a bit of trouble taking the rare losing streak in stride, one might consider those

Yankees fans to embody the characteristics of the mainstream front-runner almost by default. Therefore, it seems fair to also attribute to Yankee fans what Queenan cites as "the core emotional deficiency in the front-runner's psyche: his failure to comprehend that the thrill of victory is made a million times sweeter by the memory of defeat."[31] As this would seem to hold true for the most dedicated hometown Yankee fan that has lived her entire life in the Bronx just as much as it would for the team's most peripheral bandwagon fan from wherever, I'm left wondering if it's even worthwhile to bother with this distinction when dealing with the Yankee fanbase. Recalling Blythe's notion that there are two kinds of Americans, and that they stand as analogs for two kinds of college basketball fans, it's easy to extend that analogy to include the difference between the authentic hometown fan and the casual bandwagoner. But the analogy could be extended even further, to articulate an essential difference between New Yorkers and the rest of us to the west of the Hudson River. We're not just cheering for different teams. We're cheering for different conceptions of fandom itself, rooted in two distinct conceptions of American virtue. Pretty heady stuff, this. And it's probably of little concern to many of those baseball fans who revel in Yankee hatred. For them, the devil is truly in the details.

Chapter 5

IT'S ABOUT A MILLION
LITTLE THINGS

Okay, maybe there aren't literally a million little things that generate Yankee hatred among baseball fans. But the list of reasons for this widespread epidemic of abhorrence certainly extends beyond the previously cited areas of the players, the system, and the fans. While these three broadly drawn categories represent major obsessions for Yankee haters, excluding the quirky quips that sometimes seem to bubble up from the fans' collective unconscious would paint a picture of Yankee hatred that is misleadingly neat and tidy. So, let's take a look at some of the odds and ends that might flesh out our understanding of why so many fans have come to hate the most revered team in Major League Baseball.

First, it stands to reason that a team as successful as the Yankees would generate a good deal of animosity among fans based on specific team rivalries. Perhaps no other team in Major League Baseball is responsible for dashing the championship hopes of fans to a greater degree than the team that has won 26 World Series championships, so it was especially sweet for fans of the Arizona Diamondbacks when their team put an end to the most recent era of Yankee dominance in the Fall Classic. Diamondbacks fan Bizz12 sums up the feeling succinctly:

> There is a rivalry between the Yankees and D-Backs, courtesy of the second best World Series of all time. I was glad there finally was a team that stopped the Yankees' run at the top.[1]

Undoubtedly, this sentiment extended beyond Diamondbacks fans to the hordes of Yankee haters within the fanbase of every team outside the Bronx. While the vast majority of fans in Arizona and elsewhere were undoubtedly gracious in their celebration of Goliath's fall in 2001, the thrill of that victory was not enough to fully erase the enduring residue of Yankee hatred. In fact, it seems to have generated fresh expressions of Yankee hatred in the relatively new Diamondbacks fanbase:

> As for me, my contempt for the Yankees goes back to the 2001 World Series. Every single one of the players and coaches oozes with arrogance and self importance. You could tell by their body language and their facial expressions that they all felt the young Diamondbacks were unworthy of being in their presence. They were all so sure it would be a no-brainer win for the Yankees. When Arizona proved them all wrong, it just seemed like the national sports media and news decided that Arizona no longer existed. The level of coverage the Diamondbacks received for their historical and breathtaking win pales in comparison to that of all previous World Series winners, and the blatant disrespect continues today.[2]

This comment from Diamondbacks fan SarBear seems to sprout from the same seed that gives life to any number of small-market Yankee haters with longer histories. Even when the Yankees' swaggering hegemony is interrupted, some off-field aspect of the system manages to rain on the victory parade. But while SarBear's expression of contempt borne of small-market victimhood fits the formula well with its earnest and heartfelt tone, Diamondbacks fan Dbaxpwnall manages to cloak his own Yankee hatred in mocking ridicule:

> I love the Yankmees!!! Because of their lack of ability to close out the most important game in the season, we have a World Series championship under our belt. I also love the fact that they spend so much money every single year and, since 2000, have nothing to show for it. What's not to love? They are great for a laugh every time they lose a game. They gave me one of the fondest memories I have ever had. I still laugh every time I watch Game Seven. I laugh even harder when I watch Game Six and after the game the look on Jeter's face when they played *New York, New York*. Priceless. Like he was gonna do something about it. Why hate the Yankmees? They are great for a laugh.[3]

Certainly, postseason competition tends to generate very memorable and emotional reactions against the seemingly ever-present Yankees. But fans of teams that slog through a regular-season schedule featuring an abundance of intra-divisional Yankee games can verify that familiarity truly does breed contempt:

They [the Yankees] are a division rival. It really doesn't matter what the makeup of the team is, or the current ownership or any of them. My team, the Orioles, plays them 18 times a year and, by definition, that makes them enemy #1. Even if the Yankees were to never post 40 wins again for the next ten years and their fans become so humble they won't even come outside of their houses, I will still not like them.[4]

This expression of Yankee hatred by Schwender7 seems firmly grounded in the present. The fact that the Yankees were in his face on a regular basis last year and will be again this year defines them negatively, regardless of the actual threat they represent. Other Orioles fans, like Willym, adopt a more longitudinal path in the development of their hatred:

My loyalty to the Orioles was formed during the late 1950s and early 60s, a time period when the Yankees were winning nine AL pennants in ten years. It was a very frustrating time to be a fan of the Orioles or any other AL team. It seemed that it didn't matter what the Orioles did, because the Yankees would always win out in the end. When the Orioles finally came out on top in '66, the fact that the Yankees hit rock bottom (tenth place in a ten-team league) added considerable extra spice to my enjoyment of the year.[5]

Still other Orioles fans, like Lynnrd, feel compelled to cast their Yankee hatred as having almost primeval origins as distant as the dawn of Major League Baseball itself:

The Yankees were originally the Orioles. They moved to NYC in 1901 and became the Highlanders, and then the Yankees. It's like hating the Colts for moving to India-no-place [Indianapolis] or the [fans of the Cleveland] Browns hating us for stealing the Ravens.[6]

We can certainly forgive Lynnrd for predating the team's 1903 move to New York by a couple of years.[7] But for fans of any sport, it seems that what was true then remains true today. The movement of a franchise from one city to another is not a mere business decision; it is theft, and fans with good memories have no problem holding a grudge.

Other expressions of Yankee hatred based in specific team rivalries are more parenthetical and quick-hitting than those shared by Orioles and Diamondbacks fans. Travelingmsfan1, a Seattle Mariners fan posting to the Chicago White Sox Message Boards, offers this typical salvo:

I am a Mariners fan and I hate the Yankees. Why? Two thousand and 2001 are the biggest reasons, the two years the Yankees knocked my team out of the playoffs. Two thousand one especially gets me with the chants of "overrated" at the Stadium during the American League Championship Series, plus the racist T-shirts against Ichiro.[8]

While the specific content of incidental crowd chants can be difficult to verify, documentation of the T-shirts to which Travelingmsfan1 refers does exist. During games at Yankee Stadium in that series in 2001, some fans in attendance wore T-shirts emblazoned with the image of a fireman urinating on Mariners' outfielder Ichiro Suzuki, a player of Japanese descent. Whether this is an expression of racism, Yankee pride, or post-9/11 solidarity with first responders is a matter of opinion. However, the Mariners seemed to take umbrage, as the Yankees' visit to Seattle's Safeco Field the following spring was occasioned by an official request that fans wearing "Yankees Suck" T-shirts turn them inside-out, cover them, remove them, or leave the ballpark. Recalling those Ichiro T-shirts, Mariners' spokeswoman Rebecca Hale took the opportunity to engage in a bit of Yankee bashing of her own, stating "That was apparently appropriate at Yankee Stadium. It wouldn't be at Safeco Field."[9] One can only wonder how Ms. Hale's politically correct sensibilities might deal with a T-shirt spotted by Orioles fan Lynnrd, which bore the following historical reference: "Even Jesus Christ Hates the Yankees."[10]

Perhaps due to the wound being older and more distant in memory, a more philosophical tone pervades the following comment from Phillies fan Thelocal9, who references the Yankees' special relationship with the Kansas City Athletics mentioned earlier in this writing:

> Another reason to hate the Yanks, though, is because they were partially responsible for the A's leaving Philly. My understanding of the story is that when the Mack family was selling the team, there were two potential buyers—one that wanted to keep the team here, and another that wanted to move the team to KC. The Yanks wouldn't give approval for the Mack family to sell to the Philly group. As it turned out, the Yanks had ties to the KC group, and the KC Athletics became a de facto farm team for the Yankees in the 1950s. All of this occurred before my time. I wonder if a lot of us would have been A's fans if they had stayed here, or if the Phils would have moved at some point.[11]

It's almost as if Thelocal9 resents these actions taken by the Yankees prior to his own fandom because they prevented him from participating in what might have been a multigenerational tradition for Philadelphia baseball fans, with grandparents, parents, sons, and daughters sharing cherished merchandise and memories. Oddly, no criticism of the arrangement arises in narratives of Yankee hatred shared among fans in Kansas City. Perhaps those fans were somewhat relieved when the underperforming A's left town and the Kansas City Royals eventually proved a more successful object of their affections. It seems that memories of the Philadelphia Athletics' demise are simply too far removed from the consciousness of current-day Oakland A's fans, who also failed to include this item in their panoply of Yankee hatred.

The attraction of fandom as an expression of family tradition represents another minor thread in the phenomenon of Yankee hatred. Recall that Wann and his associates found that the most common reason for developing an identification with a team is that one's parents were fans of that team.[12] Judging from postings on the message boards, parental influence is a strong influence on Yankee hatred, as well. Washington Nationals fan Arkymark offers a characteristic reflection on this critical facet of child development:

> In my view, hating the Yankees is not limited to Red Sox fans. It is the obligation of all non-New York baseball fans everywhere and has been pretty much since Babe Ruth arrived in New York. I learned this from my mother, who was a Reds fan.[13]

Of course, as diversity in the family structure has grown concurrently with social and geographical mobility, permutations of Yankee hatred as a family tradition have increased accordingly. For example, we have the case of the child scarred from the experience of being removed from his home town and raised in Yankee country, as exemplified by Phillies fan Gophils412:

> I hate the Yankees with a burning passion. But my hate is different. It is fueled by my location, 25 miles west of NYC . . . I grew up here but was raised by relocated Philadelphians, and almost everyone in school loved the Yankees. I was always surrounded by it and this really fed my hate.[14]

Though the developmental timeline is a bit vaguer, the case of Diamondbacks fan Tigro presents a somewhat similar situation in which living as a stranger in a strange land seems to have fostered a reliance on the ties of kinship:

> I've been a Yankee hater since my interest in baseball began. That's saying a lot considering I'm a resident of New York, and that's what made a World Series like the one in '01 so sweet. It's definitely generational for me though. My dad dislikes them and my grandpa didn't care for them, either. My other grandfather didn't care for baseball all together because of teams like them.[15]

But in the presence of a passion as mighty as Yankee hatred, even family tradition can sometimes take a backseat when that family is full of Yankee fans. As evidence, I offer the case of Jerseygirl, who managed to become a

St. Louis Cardinals fan while being raised by loyal Yankees fans and living in the heart of Yankees country:

> I have disliked the Yankees most of my life. Living here in New Jersey, I get the Yankees and Mets stuffed down my throat . . . My whole family are huge Yankee fans, but they don't say much to me about it. They know I am an avid Cardinal fan and have been for many years. When they come to my home, they only see Cardinal memorabilia all over, unlike their homes with all the Yankee cr#p around.[16]

Dukeofurl, another Cardinals fan, seems to have found a way to reconcile his fandom with that of his Yankee-loving family in a less confrontational fashion, seizing the opportunity to preserve family ties when a common enemy emerges:

> I had kind of a weird, love-hate relationship with the Yankees. I hate that they seem to have a bottomless pit of money, and that Yankees/Red Sox is all that gets shown on TV anymore. But at the same time, a good chunk of my family is from Brooklyn and grew up Yankees fans, so there are the obligatory family ties. Also, after 2004, I'm obliged to cheer for anyone who's a big time rival of the Red Sox.[17]

Well, at least the need to deal with the Yankee fans in his clan allowed Dukeofurl to find a silver lining in the Cardinals' World Series defeat at the hands of the Red Sox. The case of Jerseygirl notwithstanding, Yankee hatred sometimes does take a backseat to family when that family is infested with Yankee fans. Sometimes, family obligations can result in a fan's Yankee hatred becoming a somewhat provisional notion, as is the case with Orioles fan Maui4birds:

> I've hated the Spanks forever for no particular reason, with the exception of the '78 World Series. My cousin played for them that season. That's the only time I rooted for "The Empire."[18]

Who can blame the guy for putting his hatred on hold when complimentary World Series tickets might be on the line? Surely, Maui4birds knew he could return to his hating ways the following season, when family loyalty would likely bear no personal advantage. It must be nice to have such fluidity in one's Yankee hatred, to be able to just turn it on and off at will. But for most, this kind of half-stepping is simply not an option; you're either a member of a Yankee-hating family, or you're not. Even among those who do not self-identify as Yankee haters, a little residual guilt seems to exist for not upholding the tradition. Consider the following post from Cincinnati Reds fan Johnny u:

Hate is a strong word, and hate takes effort. So, hating the Yanks isn't worth my effort. Plus, my kids are diehards (bad parenting, I suppose).[19]

Your life is your own, Johnny u, and you can live it as you see fit. But please, think of the children!

While the specifics of my online inquiry about Yankee hatred may have enticed some to comment about them, it seems reasonable to expect the pinstripes to serve as a focus for negative commentary. After all, they are, along with the interlocking "NY" logo, an immediate visual icon capable of generating immediate fan reaction. Natsfan11, a Nationals fan, picks up on my suggestion and provides a representative example of that reaction:

Now that you mention the pinstripes, I've never been a fan of pinstripes. I don't think it looks classic. To me it looks old. But for that it's not just the Yankees. I hate all the teams that have pinstripe uniforms.[20]

Well, by my unofficial count, no fewer than ten teams in Major League Baseball currently feature at least one uniform design bearing pinstripes. That's a lot of hate, Natsfan11. GnatsFan, posting to the Orioles Message Boards, but bearing a name that suggests tongue-in-cheek Washington Nationals fandom, keeps it a bit lighter with the following comment:

I once wasted two minutes of my life reading a bad Zebra joke. That's two minutes of my life I'll never get back. I've resented anything with stripes ever since.[21]

Though GnatsFan did provide the entire text of the joke in his message, I'll spare you the pain of reading it here (trust me, you've heard it before).

While holding a widely shared fashion bias against the Yankees might seem a little unjust, it's probably no more so than citing the teams' current broadcast announcers as reasons for Yankee hatred. But leave it to the fans to do just that. Perhaps it's understandable that El_Guapo, a Mets fan, is driven into a fit of pique by what he terms the Yankees' "shill announcers."[22] After all, the guy is probably a New Yorker himself, enduring constant ambient exposure to the Yankees' mouthpieces via local media all season long. But RedSoxinVt, posting to the Phillies Message Boards with a name that suggests Red Sox fandom and a Vermont zip code, includes as the seventh item in a long list of reasons to hate the Yankees "their announcer (whatever the h-3-L-L his name is) with his "ssssssssseeee yaaaaaaaaaa."[23] Well, his name is Michael Kay, and he's been the lead play-by-play voice of the Yankees on television since 2002. I understand that it's not always possible to access the hometown broadcast feed of one's favorite team when they're playing the Yankees and yes, Kay's trademark shout of "See Ya!"

following a Yankees' homer is, in my opinion, somewhat annoying. But that's because I only watch the Yankees when they're playing the Indians, and I only hear that shout when some Yankee batter takes one of the Tribe's pitchers deep into the outfield bleachers. So, here's a little advice to RedSoxinVt: do what I do—watch with the volume turned down.

The notion that jealousy is at the heart of the phenomenon of Yankee hatred has been suggested in fan comments cited in prior chapters of this writing, but only as an adjunct to some greater engine of aversion. But it's the whole ballgame for some, like Red Sox fan S FL Gio, who sums up the source of all Yankee hatred with "one word—jealousy."[24] Mets fan Poleymak is only slightly more verbose in his contention that the foundation of Yankee hatred "is jealousy in general. Who likes a team that wins all the time when yours doesn't?"[25] But Yanksfan53, posting to the Detroit Tigers Message Boards, reminds fans that the Yankees are not the only team capable of summoning the green-eyed monster with machinations aimed toward achieving dominance:

> I'm just guessing that for some people it has to do with envy. People say that the Yankees are ruining baseball by buying lots of free agents, but if it were their own General Manager that went out and got [outfielder Hideki] Matsui, Arod, [outfielder Bobby] Abreu, Damon, etc., they would be jumping for joy. For example, how many Tigers fans were excited when they got [former Marlins' infielder Miguel] Cabrera and [former Marlins' pitcher Dontrelle] Willis in the offseason? I'm sure at the time some Marlins fans despised the Tigers for "ruining baseball."[26]

While jealousy and envy of their dominance tend to be the most prevalent emotional links to Yankee hatred, fans do offer the occasional expression of pity for them, especially if their team happens to have the Yankees' number in terms of winning and losing:

> I don't hate the Yankees as much as I pity them. The Yankees are a storied franchise and, regardless of what they spend, they're good for baseball. The Yankee logo is an entity within itself. Plus we usually put the smackdown on the Yanks when we've faced off the last few years.[27]

Easy for Angels fan Travon to say, as the Yankees have been of little consequence as a barrier to his team's recent postseason aspirations. Other avenues of understanding are sometimes explored by fans willing to temper hate with rationality, as in this simple decoding of the Yankee hatred phenomenon provided by Cardinals fan Ramki:

> I tend to support the underdog in any sport, and the New York Yankees are no underdog (except maybe now, when they play the Red Sox). I'm

guessing a lot of fans out there may "hate" the Yankees while rooting for the underdog.[28]

Once again, a fan constructs a theory that frames Yankee hatred as a necessary consequence of the team's success. If everyone loves to cheer for the underdog, and the Yankees are simply too good to be considered an underdog, then they are surely doomed to be the team that everyone must hate. For fans willing to embrace this interpretation, the Yankees' hegemony and the hate it inspires can actually be construed as something that is good for baseball. Yankee hatred may actually be the key to the Yankees' popularity and centrality to the game itself.

In 1826, just four years before his death, English author William Hazlitt composed an essay titled "On the Pleasure of Hating." While there were no New York Yankees around to hate in 1826, Hazlitt's words might be considered a prescient insight into the role they now occupy in the lives of baseball fans in need of a focus for blame when their team falters:

> Nature seems (the more we look into it) made up of antipathies: without something to hate, we should lose the very spring of thought and action. Life would turn to a stagnant pool, were it not ruffled by the jarring interests, the unruly passions of men. The white streak in our own fortunes is brightened (or just rendered visible) by making all around it as dark as possible; so the rainbow paints its form upon the cloud. Is it pride? Is it envy? Is it the force of contrast? Is it weakness or malice? But so it is, that there is a secret affinity, a *hankering* after evil in the human mind, and that it takes a perverse, but a fortunate delight in mischief, since it is a never-failing source of satisfaction. Pure good soon grows insipid, wants variety and spirit. Pain is a bittersweet, which never surfeits. Love turns, with a little indulgence, to indifference or disgust: hatred alone is immortal.[29]

Like many Kansas City Royals fans, Blu4evr sounds like someone whose love of the home team might turn to indifference or disgust if not for a singular object of hatred like the Yankees:

> I think that if you have a favorite team, you almost need a tangible enemy for that team. The twenty-nine teams in Major league Baseball are too varied to hate altogether, and if I'm going to pick an arch-nemesis (albeit one that dwarfs our talent), I want it to be the one that resembles a *Star Wars*-esque evil empire. And who better for that role than the franchise that has everything?[30]

Testimony that today's baseball fan yearns for something evil in which to find that perverse and consistent satisfaction Hazlitt cites, and that this evil something is the New York Yankees, is offered up by Reds fan Ogredsfan:

They are a blast to hate. But I'd hate to think of the state of MLB without them. *Star Wars*, an overrated film to begin with, would have been a complete snore without Darth Vader.[31]

While both Blu4evr and Ogredsfan are undoubtedly devoted fans of their respective teams, each clearly feels that his enjoyment of fandom is enhanced by Yankee hatred. A true fan may feel as if she is in heaven when actively rooting for her team. But Blu4evr and Ogredsfan might be quick to remind her of a cautionary lyric sung by David Byrne of the band Talking Heads, which echoes Hazlitt's view: "Heaven is a place where nothing ever happens."[32] But add some detestation to the mix, and we're in business.

Recall that in his privileging of pity over hatred in his own reaction to the Yankees, Angels fan Travon bolstered his view with the claim that, regardless of the vast sums of money they spend, the Yankees are good for baseball. Many have advanced this argument for the Yankees' worth on economic terms, claiming that other teams' revenue streams are enhanced whenever the Yankees come to town due to the influx of haters at the turnstiles. While A's fan Salbando6 concurs, his comments indicate that the role played by the Yankees in the lives of fans extends beyond giving their home team the occasional financial boost. Hazlitt opined that "public nuisances are in the nature of public benefits."[33] Indeed, hating the Yankees, perhaps as much as loving the home team, can be the glue that binds a community of fans together:

> I think baseball fans look forward to the Yankees' annual spending spree so they have something to talk about. The Yankees would be boring if they didn't do this . . . The $200 million contracts make news, which results in more ticket sales. "OMG, look at what Arod gets paid now. No one is worth that. Let's get tickets and boo the hell out of him when he comes to the plate." If you don't believe me, look at the Yankees' attendance numbers in Oakland, and then compare that to the Rays, Royals, etc. They certainly aren't there because their Grandpa liked or hated Mickey Mantle.[34]

Within many of these overt expressions of hatred, there is a certain measure of respect for this singular role that the Yankees play for fans of those other 29 teams, and Tigers fan Ty mccobb actually summons the courage to publicly speak its name:

> I have always "hated" the Yankees, but mostly out of respect. One of my best buddies is a born-and-raised-in-Michigan Yankee fan, so we rag on each other, respectfully. They are the most historic sports franchise ever. So, like most Yankee haters, I do it out of sports-respect.[35]

It's like what Hazlitt said regarding his lack of will to crush a spider crawling across the floor, despite his hatred of the very sight of it:

> The spirit of malevolence survives the practical exertion of it. We learn to curb our will and keep our overt actions within the bounds of humanity, long before we can subdue our sentiments and imaginations to the same mild tone. We give up the external demonstration, the *brute* violence, but cannot part with the essence or principle of hostility.[36]

Not all Yankee haters are quite so philosophical about their animosity. Some, like RedSoxinVt, whose complaint about the Yankees' play-by-play announcer was mentioned earlier, revel in the minutiae of long lists of specific, odious offenses. Others, like Mojo32, view such a cataloguing of details as unnecessary for explaining something so self-evident:

> I'm a Red Sox fan and a D'backs fan. So, yes, I despise the Yankees. There should be no explanation why.[37]

Every Yankee hater has his reasons, and those reasons have become a part of every Yankee hater; they are inseparable from their identity as baseball fans, regardless of the team they call their own. Given this condition, asking fans to objectively explain their Yankee hatred through some form of self-analysis might be asking a bit too much. So, in this investigation of Yankee hatred, the time has come to step away from the gripes of the dedicated fan, step in to the role of analyst, and try to determine what it's really about.

Chapter 6

WHAT IT'S REALLY ABOUT

We've examined the phenomenon of Yankee hatred from a variety of perspectives: animosity grounded in fans' perceptions of players associated with the Yankees, the notion that the Yankees and Major League Baseball constitute an alliance that produces systemic unfairness, the perceived attitude of Yankee fans and New Yorkers in general, and an assortment of complaints numerous and diverse enough to warrant the catch-all category found in the last chapter. In all cases, comments drawn from fan narratives have provided ample evidence that these are active concerns in the lives of a broad spectrum of baseball fans representing every team fanbase in Major League Baseball. While characterized by a high degree of honesty, humor, and passion, these narratives cannot fully account for the origins of Yankee hatred, nor can they fully explain how it functions, or what purpose it serves, in the lives of those fans. So ingrained in their subjective fan experience is the phenomenon of Yankee hatred that a sufficiently objective consideration of these issues simply might not be available to them. Though I, too, am a baseball fan in whom a healthy degree of Yankee hatred has taken root, it now falls upon me to attempt to step outside my fandom in order to assess the origin, function, and purpose of that hatred. To assist me in this unlikely task, I will enlist the wisdom of others who have dedicated their intellectual lives to understanding fandom, but are likely to do so from a position of greater distance from off-season concerns about filling that hole at third base or the nail-biting anxiety that accompanies a late-season push for the playoffs.

Before addressing the specific negativity implied by Yankee hatred, let's examine the more generally positive project of distinction generated by fandom for one's favorite team. In the first chapter of this book, I mentioned the possible dangers of accepting fans' narratives as objective knowledge of their fandom. My reason for addressing this potential problem was not to suggest that what passes for fan knowledge is somehow deficient in its content or accuracy, but rather to advance the idea that disinterested analysis might be required in order to make objective sense of the unique mix of information and passion found in these fan narratives. Indeed, I absorbed a great deal of objective knowledge about Yankee hatred by reading these fan narratives. Still, those same readings reveal a blend of emotion, fantasy, and rational thought that loses much of its impact if one splits those constituent parts from one another in an attempt to isolate objective knowledge about Yankee hatred. It is certainly a curious trait of many baseball fans that they bring encyclopedic reservoirs of statistical data and historical erudition to an enterprise that is, when all is said and done, just a diversionary entertainment. In order to best comprehend this sort of fandom, I would like to follow the examples set by Hills, Sandvoss, and other scholars of fan culture in referencing an approach that accepts fandom's mix of the rational and the emotional as whole cloth, refusing to privilege one over the other. That approach finds its source in the work of child psychologist D. W. Winnicott.

Now, employing the work of a child psychologist in order to examine the thought and behavior of adult baseball fans might be seen as condescending or insulting. After all, most of these folks seem to be responsible, intelligent members of society, not a bunch of screaming kids waiting to be picked up from the daycare center. But Winnicott's account of the role of play in the psychological development of the child can shed a great deal of light on what might be considered a playful side in the lives of otherwise serious, productive men and women. In his 1951 paper, "Transitional Objects and Transitional Phenomena," Winnicott develops the concept of the *transitional object* as a central component of infant development through play.[1] Initially existing within a state of wholeness in which the self and the external world are completely merged, the infant eventually endures experiences that highlight a lack of omnipotence and control over that state of wholeness, which serves as the motivation for the development of a self. The key to managing this development of an inner sense of self distinct from external reality is the transitional object, which serves as the infant's first "me/not me" object. Acting as a bridge between the inner and outer worlds, the transitional object can be a teddy bear, a blanket, or any soft, pliable object that is accessible to the infant and appropriate for sucking, fondling, and comforting. The specific object used is far less important than the way it is used, namely as a possession that the infant feels she simultaneously finds and creates, with this possession belonging to an external reality and having physical characteristics all its own, but being manipulated and controlled in service to her personal comfort. Through the use of such a transitional object, the infant opens up a new realm of experience that does not comprise either the inner reality of the self or the outer reality of the external world. Winnicott maintains that this third realm is where the infant plays with inner and outer realities, keeping them separate when necessary and experimentally relating them when growth opportunities are present. This use of the transitional object as a bridging and separation agent requires it to be a physical object, rather than some figment of the infant's fully self-contained imagination, so that the infant may have material evidence that the world is not just something he perceives, but something he actively structures. This sense of active control is also why the transitional object must not be removed or changed by anyone except the infant. Many parents have witnessed the ear-splitting objections registered when, no longer able to stand those nasty stains and smells, they try to sneak that security blanket off to the laundry room for a quick wash. For the infant, it's not about cleanliness; it's about a complete loss of control over the one object that can mediate the relationship between the self and the external world.

But what can this use of transitional objects by infants tell us about baseball fans, very few of whom seem to be infants? According to Winnicott, an infant's use of a transitional object eventually results in a sort of diffusion of that object into the external realm of culture, once it has served its developmental purpose in the child's life. In other words, the teddy bear that enabled the infant to develop is replaced by art, religion, and other cultural institutions through which an adult might find a confluence of the inner self and outer society later in life. It's conceivable that one such cultural practice occupying the adult space formerly reserved for the infant's transitional objects might be fandom. In his review of a study of soap opera fans conducted by C. Lee Harrington and Denise Bielby, Hills acknowledges the mediating power of transitional objects as a central feature of the appeal of this popular entertainment genre:

> Through affective play, soap opera becomes a "transitional object" for its fans. Soap texts therefore no longer belong purely in "external reality," nor are they entirely taken in to the fans' "internal reality." Instead these texts can be used creatively by fans to manage tensions between inner and outer worlds. If any one of us became caught up purely in our inner world of fantasy then we would effectively become psychotic; if we had no sense of a vibrant inner world and felt entirely caught up in "external" reality then, conversely, we would lack a sense of our own uniqueness and

our own self . . . It is therefore of paramount importance for mental health
that our inner and outer worlds do not stray too far from one another, and
that they are kept separate but also interrelated . . . It is also important to
realise that this process is ongoing and does not correspond to a childhood
activity which adults are somehow not implicated in. All of us, throughout
our lives, draw on cultural artefacts as "transitional objects."[2]

There's little reason to assume that what is thought to be true for the soap
opera fan is not also true for the sports fan. For members of both fan
groups, the object of fandom resembles an adult version of an infant's
transitional object in that it is something ostensibly used as a plaything to
occupy leisure time. Additionally, it seems that the object of fandom is, in
both cases, used to mediate the fan's inner world and the outer world of external reality, allowing for the appropriate maintenance of their separation
while providing opportunities for the realization of their interrelatedness
in a newly created transitional space. The sports fan, like the soap opera
fan, surely realizes that the object of his fandom constitutes a "me/not me"
object; he knows that he did not really create it and that it exists prior to his
own appreciation of it, while simultaneously recognizing that his personal
fandom is a personal project that yields a relationship which is unique and
distinct from that of other fans of the same object. But should we assume
that these expressions of adult fandom are simply grown-up versions of a
baby hugging a teddy bear? If so, is it fair to ask why all of those supposedly mature adults at the ballpark are acting like a bunch of babies? Is their
fandom really a sort of infantile regression, an avoidance of the need to do
something a bit more productive with their time? Shouldn't they grow up
already?

Hills addresses this popular complaint about adult fandom by insisting
that a distinction be made between what he terms the "proper transitional
object," or *pto*, of childhood and the external realm of cultural institutions and practices into which it diffuses and which, in turn, becomes an
appropriate place for mediating the inner self and the external world in
adulthood. Noting that Winnicott was a bit vague regarding how privately
sucking on a blanket in the crib is displaced by a public appreciation of a
new exhibit at the art museum, Hills argues against any assumption that
the personal pleasures of infancy and the communal pleasures of adult
culture must be focused on different objects. In fact, he implies that it is
more likely that the fandom accompanying contemporary popular culture
would find its focus in objects that appeal to both children and adults:

A fan culture is formed around any given text when this text has functioned
as a *pto* in the biography of a number of individuals; individuals who
remain attached to this text by virtue of the fact that it continues to exist as

an element of their cultural experience. Unlike the inherently private but also externally objective *pto*, this "retained" object must negotiate its intensely subjective significance with its intersubjective cultural status. It is this essential tension which marks it out as a *secondary transitional object*.[3]

It's probably not too difficult for sports fans to see their own fandom reflected in this notion of the secondary transitional object. Initially, our sports fandom is often developed in childhood, and characterized by the sort of private fantasizing that accompanies an infant's relationship to a blanket, teddy bear, or other *pto*. We're clearly in that third realm described by Winnicott, where we're imagining that we're making that diving catch, or hitting that walk-off homer, all the while coming to terms with the knowledge that it's not really us but, rather, an idealized professional athlete who's doing it all. While growing up may signal the end of this projection of desires onto actual players, it certainly does not signal an end to our fandom. Indeed, we retain that fandom for our favorite team as a secondary transitional object, one that isn't so much privately played with, as in our childhood fantasies, but one that is now shared with a fanbase as a communal experience that includes fond remembrances of our original childhood connection. This comingling of the private affective power of fandom derived from its original use as a proper transitional object and its secondary role as a shared cultural experience is reflected whenever fans speak in terms of how "we" won last night. In reality, the adult in us knows it was "they" who won, "they" being the players contracted by some wealthy team owner to perform athletic tasks on the field while wearing matching uniforms. Yet, we continue to negotiate peace between these dual natures of our fandom for as long as we remain fans. Of course, not all fans were there during childhood, but the fact that some become fans well into their adult lives is evidence that this third realm can be accessed and used for the mediation of self and outer reality by those who already have a fully developed sense of self. That they can simply jump on board at the level of communal experience without having internalized their fandom though its use as a transitional object in childhood speaks to fandom's ability to reside in both individual psychology and the cultural field.

Of course, not every transitional childhood object presents itself as an appropriate candidate for retention and use as a secondary transitional object within adult cultural experience. Clearly, drool-soaked blankets would constitute an unlikely object class for adult fandom. Such items are simply too personal in nature, deriving their status as proper transitional objects in a context where the infant is not even aware of their commodity function within a market-driven economic system. Truly, it's the rare infant who would be present for, and aware of, the retail purchase of their transitional object from a store shelf containing scores of identical, mass-produced units. More likely, that infant would encounter that transitional object as a serendipitous discovery; something that just appears in the world around him and is claimed and refashioned as his own. This realm of the openly commodified object attracts more likely candidates for retention as the secondary transitional object of mature fandom. While some of these commodities are targeted toward an exclusively youthful audience, others are clearly structured in a manner designed to appeal to both children and adults. Anyone who has watched, say, an episode of *The Simpsons* with a young child has surely experienced the mild discomfort of thinking they'll have to come up with a child-friendly way to decode one of the oh-so-adult references with which that program is routinely peppered, only to find that the kid was thoroughly engrossed in the program's tamer elements, while the edgier stuff blew right by them. Our current popular culture is replete with commodified entertainment featuring this sort of double coding, creating a vast reservoir of potential fan objects capable of bridging the child-to-adult audience gap. Major League Baseball seems to rest comfortably in this reservoir, offering age-appropriate pleasures for both kids and adults, resulting in far greater staying power than other more age-specific items. Indeed, while many popular culture commodities are structured with a planned obsolescence prominent enough to force a child's disinterest in them before they can even be fully utilized as proper transitional objects, baseball represents a fan object of unusually high quality and durability, offering the possibility of an almost cradle-to-grave fan commitment. For example, while some of the toys unwrapped on Christmas morning are quickly jettisoned in favor of the box in which they were packaged, it's not uncommon for a baseball glove received in childhood to become a treasured icon of a lifelong connection to the game.

But can an object of fandom with this much staying power result in a fan becoming hopelessly mired in it, unable to move beyond an exclusive and obsessive attachment every bit as dysfunctional as the preempted relationship between a developing child and last week's hot toy? Hills may offer an answer to this question in his suggestion that the secondary transitional object of adult fandom might best be thought of not as an object, per se, but as an individualized version of Winnicott's playful third realm between inner self and outer reality, which "cannot be viewed as synonymous with 'culture,' religion or art *tout court* but should be perceived instead as a region of 'personalised' culture."[4] Noting Winnicott's claim that phenomena within this third realm are characterized by a sort of limitless variability in regard to their use as objects of play, Hills suggests that this variability may explain why fans often seem so obsessively attached to the same old thing.[5] After all, if a fan can endlessly refashion and play with their beloved object of fandom, negotiating an endlessly evolving and productive third realm of meaning, who cares if disinterested non-fans think they're just spinning their wheels? Still, it seems reasonable to expect that even the most optimistic fan of a winning team might get a little bored with all that seamless positivity, no matter how clever their third-realm activities may be. Wann and his associates, borrowing from market research on disposition theory that reveals a positive correlation between positive consumer attitudes and product purchase, have identified research on sport spectators suggesting a different consumption dynamic:

> Disposition theory states that not only do spectators enjoy watching their favorite team play well, but they also gain great satisfaction observing a despised team being humiliated . . . Consequently, sport fans consume sport not only when they hold a favorable attitude toward the product (i.e., their favorite team is playing), but, in some instances, when they hold negative attitudes (i.e., when a despised team is playing).[6]

If fans that attain a positive mental state from watching their own team's victories can find additional satisfaction watching a despised team lose, just imagine how important watching that despised team fail must be for fans that support a loser. For those seeking the maximum level of satisfaction from their fan experience, it appears that simply reveling in a favorite team's victories is not enough. Could one byproduct of all that endless variability available to fans as they creatively play within their little regions of personalized culture be the construction of an enjoyable hatred? Could the copiously documented phenomenon of Yankee hatred allow a fan to gain a higher degree of satisfaction by occasionally unmooring herself from all that positive rooting for the home team? Is that what this is all about?

Although he was not all that interested in baseball fans, Winnicott revealed a possible path for the formation of a fanbase in his contention that an infant's social development hinges on the illusions constructed by the infant through imaginative play within that third realm of transitional phenomena:

> We can share a respect for *illusory experience*, and if we wish we may collect together and form a group on the basis of the similarity of our illusory experiences. This is a natural root of grouping among human beings.[7]

In other words, fans of a given team may be individually engaged in the illusory experience of constructing some sort of relationship between themselves and the team that serves as the object of their fandom, and recognition of that illusory relationship in others might enable the creation of some sort of socially organized fanbase. Of course, it is assumed that any such social organization of fandom must be a rather spontaneous and consensual occurrence, and that fans of different teams must respect each other's team-specific illusory projects of fandom. For example, Tigers fans and Twins fans can share a mutual respect for each other's passion and loyalty to their team, but it's not as if Tigers fans can legitimately proselytize the Twins fanbase in order to gain converts to the Tigers' cause. Winnicott explicitly cautions against such an aggressive extension of one's personal, subjective transitional space into the lives of others:

> Should an adult make claims on us for our acceptance of the objectivity of his subjective phenomena we discern or diagnose madness. If, however, the adult can manage to enjoy the personal intermediate area without making claims, then we can acknowledge our own corresponding intermediate areas, and are pleased to find a degree of overlapping.[8]

One product of this overlap is the not uncommon position of being a fan of the game first and a fan of a particular team second. After all, the history, lore, and institutional structure of professional baseball represent common ground for fans of all teams. Even specific team rivalries are part of this community property, an enjoyable feature of the game that boosts interest and binds fans together in a celebration of friendly competition. But as suggested earlier, there is no rule that all of this overlapping has to be expressed in such affectionate terms. Indeed, Yankee hatred represents an area of overlap that impacts every fanbase in Major League Baseball outside the Bronx.

The symbiotic relationship between love for one's team and hatred of the Yankees suggested by Winnicott's work stands in contrast to the Kleinian approach to fandom mentioned in the first chapter of this book. Based on the notion of the paranoid-schizoid position, in which an infant splits good feelings from the bad ones and projects the latter onto the mother in order to preserve the uncontaminated good within the self, the Kleinian approach paints a comparatively dismal picture of psychic development as a struggle between the good self and those repressive elements that have been violently expelled—elements that seem to haunt the psyche as the infant gradually comes to view the mother, who now contains them, as an autonomous source of both good and bad. This view does provide a reasonable explanation of the sometimes painful process through which a child develops a less projection-oriented method of relating to external objects. In fact, the Kleinian approach seems to suggest that experiencing these anxieties is essential for the development of responsibility, guilt, and a host of other moral capacities that are indicative of psychological health and maturity. It's easy to see how this model could be applied to adult baseball fans who might be viewed as projecting bad feelings onto rival teams while preserving the good by associating it with their own team, using this contrast as a means of continually refining their fandom as an extension of the developing self. But the Kleinian approach doesn't seem to fully account for the pleasure fans clearly derive from their Yankee hatred. Rather than accepting it as a vehicle for reaching the endpoint of a painful, yet necessary phase of personal development, it seems that most Yankee haters want the hate to live forever as a treasured aspect of their fandom. The lexicon of Kleinian psychology even refers to this stage of development as the *depressive position*, a term which clearly implies that those experiencing this stage might want it to be resolved as quickly as possible. However, this is simply not the case among those who revel in the eternal joys of Yankee hatred. For these reasons, Winnicott's vision of infinite play within a third realm of fan objects used as transitional phenomena seems to offer a better explanation of Yankee hatred's role in the lives of fans, as the Kleinian model would likely frame the endless joy of Yankee hatred as a regressive and dysfunctional enterprise engaged in by those who simply refuse to mature and move on.

So, how should one view these otherwise normative, fully functioning adult members of society who flourish in an imaginary playground in which a particular kind of hate plays an integral part in their beloved project of fandom? While acknowledging the usefulness of Hills' appropriation of Winnicottian principles, Sandvoss offers a somewhat different take on the psychological underpinnings of adult fandom. It seems that some of that difference can be traced to Hills' observation that the most likely products of popular culture for conversion into objects of fandom are those that appeal to both children and adults. Baseball, as already noted, seems to fit into that product class, with fandom extending to those who have retained associations with it, which they formed in childhood, as well as to those who have discovered it in adulthood as part of the broader cultural realm. But Sandvoss, responding to Hills' argument that continued association with favored childhood objects constitutes a form of nostalgia, rather than fandom, revisits the notions of proper and secondary transitional objects in a manner that yields a different, yet largely complementary, explanation of purely adult fandom.[9] Preferring to leave open the possibility that fandom retained from childhood involves the potentially regressive retention of proper transitional objects, Sandvoss proposes an alternative to the secondary transitional object theory that is so central to Hills' explanation of adult fandom. Specifically, he proposes a vision of adult fandom grounded in a narcissistic extension of the self, rather than in the secondary transitional object Hills equates with a realm of personalized cultural activity.

Sandvoss notes an obvious duality of fandom in his observation that its object is distant and separate, even though the fan feels that he is engaged with it. The perception that such an external object can accurately reflect cherished qualities of the developed adult self, and that the self can reciprocate by reflecting the preferred qualities of the object, constitutes the narcissistic foundation of adult fandom. For Sandvoss, this narcissistic self-reflection occurs not just between like-minded individual fans, but extends to the relationship between individual fans and the material objects of fandom. Just as Narcissus compulsively gazed at his reflection in the water, fans are fascinated by any extension of themselves that they perceive in material existing outside themselves.[10] In this way, objects of fandom can be seen as transcending their role as transitional objects used to negotiate a balance between the inner self and outer reality, becoming constituent parts of the self. If these external objects of fandom were completely accurate reflections of the fan's true self, this narcissism would seem completely benign. But these external objects are changeable; they are not controlled by the fan, but by the popular culture industry that manages them. As fan objects become increasingly central to a fan's self identity, Sandvoss warns that any change in those objects creates a condition in which "the object of fandom as extension of self is privileged over the self."[11] In other words, it is possible that the fan's conception of self is not reflected in, but defined by, the consumer merchandise related to the object of fandom. Similarly, the everyday life of the fan may be interpreted as a narcissistic public performance of this commodified self. How else to explain that guy running on to the playing field, proudly wearing a replica of his team's official jersey, who achieves a cheerful state of euphoria when his display of superfandom is met with the perfunctory chase and arrest? Of course, such attempts to actually achieve the fame and celebrity of the fan object can be considered dysfunctional exceptions to the rule of fans fulfilling their narcissism through mere self-identification with that fan object. This more normative expression of fandom routinely involves the projection of self-identity onto a collective, resulting in a healthier sense of belonging that balances fandom's construction of self and community. In this form, fandom seems to generate an emotional response similar to that associated with the place we call home, or what Sandvoss refers to as "the form of physical, emotional *and* ideological space that is best described as *Heimat*."[12]

A term of German origin, Heimat evokes all of the comforting, secure features one traditionally associates with home. Recall the distinction that Blythe makes between what he considers to be two types of Americans: those modern denizens of the urban landscape for whom home is little more than a crash-pad, and those for whom home signifies a permanence that can be shed no more easily than one might shed their own skin. It is this latter conception of home as an organic component of one's being to which the term Heimat refers. Fans often reflect the importance of actual physical space, as identified by this concept of Heimat, in their references to the home-like atmosphere they perceive when seated in one of those excruciatingly uncomfortable stadium chairs. So profoundly felt is this notion of stadium-as-home that some fans openly express a desire to have their ashes scattered on their team's field of play in order to be eternally ensconced in the one place to which they feel an inextricable linkage. But the permanence suggested by this traditional interpretation of Heimat can inform modern fandom only to a point, as many objects of fandom provide no connection to physical territory whatsoever. Consider the myriad fan-bases dedicated to television shows, cult films, and other art forms based on fictional narratives. Where is the Heimat in this sort of fandom? Sand-voss suggests updating the traditional conception of Heimat in order to accommodate its application to those spaces in which a great deal of modern fandom is evident:

> These spaces differ from the territorial place conventionally understood as *Heimat* . . . They can be physical as well as textual, and hence can be accessed by fans in different mediated and unmediated ways, at different times, and from different localities. The sense of home in fandom is in fact a mobile *Heimat*.[13]

While baseball fans may interpret their team's stadium as one of those physical places that are central to traditional Heimat, there can be no doubt that they also employ the type of mobile Heimat crucial to fan expression, but focused on purely fictional texts. The need for this mobile version of Heimat in the lives of baseball fans is perhaps necessitated by the increasingly mobile nature of society itself. In the current era, it would seem virtually impossible for a team's fanbase to be maintained if fandom required one's permanent physical presence, from cradle to grave, in the city hosting that team. Old fans leave town, and new fans move in, but the generation and maintenance of fandom for the home team can exist for both groups. I can personally attest to this as an Indians fan that has not lived anywhere near Cleveland for a quarter century. Indeed, the constant maintenance of my Indians fandom has become an even more important project since moving away, as it constitutes one of the few remaining personal connections to what will always be my home town. I can also attest to the fragility of such connections to place through a past object of fandom, the Cleveland Browns of the National Football League. That I am no longer a Browns fan is clearly a function of my absence from the team's physical location during their departure from Cleveland and their resurrection as the Baltimore Ravens in 1996. Though the city of Cleveland would receive an expansion franchise named the Browns in 1999, the severing of my original fandom constituted the severing of an irreparable personal linkage, and I have been unable to think of these new Browns as anything other than imposters. Had I still lived in the Cleveland area, perhaps I could have reconstituted that linkage in a way that honored the qualities of traditional Heimat I once felt. But at that point, attempting to become a fan of the new Browns would have seemed as disrespectful to my original fandom as an attempt to refashion myself as a Steelers fan. Still, as tragic as this loss has been, there is an upside: my Sunday afternoons are now a lot more productive.

The case of my lost Browns fandom is a rather peculiar one, generated by the twin quirks of personal and franchise relocation. Far more common is the phenomenon of fans maintaining their allegiances despite their physical relocation, as well as the construction of new fans, regardless of their geographical histories. This mobile Heimat of fandom accounts for both phenomena. In his interpretation of fanbases as imagined communities, Crawford bolsters the notion of a mobile Heimat by observing that the warmth and supportiveness of actual physical communities is in increasingly short supply, and that sports fandom is becoming an increasingly common substitute source of group identity and togetherness.[14] While this substitution effect might be most directly experienced through attendance at an actual sports venue, Crawford emphasizes that the team's role as a representative of a specific geographic locality is only the beginning, as its fanbase may ultimately extend far beyond its home city. This is not meant to imply that physical locality has become unimportant, but rather that the traditional qualities of local community are now often imaginatively reconstructed by a team's geographically dispersed fanbase. Of course, the primary agency for these fan projects aimed at the reinvention of a local cultural ethos is the consumption of all that officially licensed team merchandise. While this focus on commodities can expose these extended fanbases to the common cultural criticism that, unlike real fans, they're just bandwagoners on a shopping spree, Crawford notes an increasing sensitivity among fandom scholars to consumption as a type of social performance, and to all that merchandise as vital resources in the construction of fan identity.[15] As suggested by the fan narratives cited earlier in this book, the New York Yankees have been a prime beneficiary of this imagined fandom, a mobile Heimat in which the décor revolves around the Yankee logo, and the cultural sensibility is infused with a New York attitude, regardless of the fan's geographical location. Yet, this process is not restricted to globally recognized superteams like the Yankees, as my own experience with baseball fandom demonstrates. After my relocation to Eastern Pennsylvania, I considered the possibility of developing a secondary fan connection to one of the more geographically proximate teams that was not in direct competition with the Tribe, such as the Phillies or the Mets. I soon realized that doing so would involve incorporating the imagined cultural ethos of one of those fanbases, as well as dropping a significant sum of money on the appropriate team gear. Though I could afford the financial investment, I just couldn't pull the trigger on morphing into someone who was culturally Philly, or culturally Queens. My lifelong investment in becoming culturally Cleveland was apparently too powerful to be overcome by the mere adoption of a new zip code. But it's not as if the opportunity is unavailable to those with lighter cultural baggage, or those looking to purchase new baggage. A global commodity supply chain ensures the possibility of Indians fans from Indianapolis to India. Yet, the question remains: what is it about the Yankees that makes them the most prolific example of this process? If this process produces legions of adoring Yankee fans, how do so many rival fans of those other 29 teams annually thrust into an antagonistic fight to the death find a common cause in their Yankee hatred?

Both Crawford, in his conception of fanbases as neo-tribes, and Sandvoss, in his view of fandom as mobile Heimat, caution against any assumption that such globally available, imagined realities constitute spaces in which just anyone is welcome to become a member. Whether we're talking about its traditional conception or the mobile version represented by modern fandom, Sandvoss would remind us that *"Heimat . . .* always involves an evaluation and categorization of others."[16] Like any of the more traditional social groupings, modern fanbases are defined by their ability to include some and exclude others. The value of a fan's inclusion in the mobile, imagined, idealized, hometown Heimat of a team's fanbase is derived precisely from the fact that so many others aren't invited to the party. While it's true that a fanbase must define itself against what it is not, a significant degree of common experience exists among the fanbases of baseball. In just about every case, despite the constant competitive veneer and intense rivalries, we all win some and lose some. We all worry about how our team will balance financial reality with the need to address all of the holes in its roster. We all dread the day we pick up the hometown paper and discover that our fervent support was just not enough to keep the team from relocating to some city with a newer stadium and hungrier fans. If the lines between fanbases were more clear-cut, if we all weren't in the same boat in regard to so many fan concerns, that need to definitively know who's with us and who's against us in our fan communities would be so much easier to satisfy. If only there were some entity in Major League Baseball that truly stood apart, a no-brainer exclusion that could provide a stark contrast and remove this ambivalence, allowing us to define our projects of fandom once and for all.

Well, say hello to the New York Yankees, a team that has won an unbelievable 26 World Series championships; a team with a fanbase and front office that considers a season resulting in anything less than a 27th to be an abject failure; a team with a seemingly limitless ability to outspend every competitor and procure the services of any player they desire; a team with a position so central to the history of baseball itself that the possibility of franchise relocation is simply unthinkable; and a team with a mass media focus that makes them the nationwide default object of consumption in sportscasting. In so many concrete ways, the Yankees are, in the eyes of every other fanbase in Major League Baseball, the undeniable other. But just as the Heimat of any fanbase is, at once, based in concrete reality and imaginatively constructed, so is the phenomenon of Yankee hatred. If some of the fan narratives of Yankee hatred contained in this book read a bit like irrational fantasies, it might help to simply view them as the creative products of fans' imaginations, for which the harsh reality of inequality in Major League Baseball is only a starting point. All of those imagined, positive qualities that comprise the Heimat of any team's fanbase find a necessary and defining counterpoint in the imagined, negative qualities resulting in the Yankees' amplified status as "imagined other."

The mixture of reality and fantasy that informs both positive team fandom and Yankee hatred is not restricted to the players on the field and the fans in the seats. It also permeates the broader cultural field, which, in turn, only serves to intensify the sport-specific phenomenon of Yankee hatred. Roger Aden uses Bourdieu's concept of a physical, material habitus to frame his argument for fans' construction of an imagined habitus in which symbolic pilgrimages can occur, creating not only a vehicle for fan interaction, but also a communal vision of a virtual reality that might inform fan consciousness to a greater degree than actual physical reality.[17] The phenomenon of Yankee hatred offers plenty of evidence that the construction of such an alternative habitus involves the aforementioned combination of real and imagined components that are so crucial to the construction of modern fandom. Many fans, regardless of their team affiliation and place of residence, have had the opportunity to visit both New York City and Yankee Stadium. Yet, any conception of these places is certainly not exclusively informed by the objective reality observed during such visits. Instead, the significance of Yankee Stadium or New York City within any Major League Baseball fanbase is the product of a melding of such primary research from the field with a plethora of mass-mediated images and narratives, nasty jokes borne of regional defensiveness, and other assorted folklore about these far-away places. Perhaps most importantly, any alternative habitus of Yankee hatred is informed by the stories fans tell one another, which comprise a veritable warehouse of mythology developed in the self-reinforcing echo chambers frequented by like-minded fans, such as the neighborhood sports bar, the couch in front of a fellow fan's television, or the message boards found on a team's Web site. Judging from the content of those message boards, the alternative habitus of Yankee hatred that thrives in each of them has as much to do with a virtual conception of a negative New York as with any negative feelings toward the Yankees in particular. In other words, that negative other against which fans construct their own identity is, at least in part, the culture of New York City, of which the Yankees are the most prominent representative in the world of the baseball fan. Just as a team's fanbase reinvents an idealized version of the local cultural ethos for which their team is a representative, that same fanbase can access a self-defining mirror-opposite through the imaginative construction of those evil Yankees and their evil city.

Hills' consideration of what he terms *cult geography* can further illuminate the role played by Yankee Stadium and New York City as physical touchstones of Yankee hatred. While acknowledging that imagined versions of reality and the reality of physical place cannot be fully merged into a seamless entity, Hills objects to the tendency of some observers to insist that the imagined and the authentically real must always remain within separate realms.[18] That the project of fandom involves some playful blurring of the boundaries of the real and the imagined is no reason to assume that fans can't tell the difference between the real world and their own fantasies. To do so would be to marginalize all fans as delusional and in dire need of psychiatric care, ignoring the obvious ability of fans to function in the real world when the game is over. Concern over this blurring of the authentic and the imaginary among fans is, to some degree, linked to concerns regarding the exploitation of fans by those who would commodify reality and sell it back to us as some sort of theme park; the nightmare scenario of folks foregoing that trip to Europe because they already saw it all at Epcot Center. To quell such concerns, Hills suggests Elvis Presley's Graceland as a more fitting example of how fans might employ cult geography:

> While the commodification of, say, Disneyland presents a space which inevitably exists in tension with the values of the originating Disney texts—hyperromantic values of child-like freedom, "magic" and sentiment—Graceland's commodification reiterates the already hyper-commodified values of its icon's own life and death. It re-presents themes and realities which are central to fans' experience of Elvis, meaning that its commodification does not represent an inherent disruption of "authentic" Elvis cultism.[19]

Consider the Yankees to be Elvis, and the physical realities of Yankee Stadium and New York City to be Graceland, and a vision of a non-delusional Yankee hatred begins to emerge. Like Elvis, the Yankees stand as a highly commodified, openly marketed entity, inextricably linked to two equally commodified locations. That Yankee haters engage in a fandom which reworks this relationship in a negative fashion, while Elvis fans on either real or symbolic pilgrimages to Graceland do so positively, should not obscure the importance of cult geography to both enterprises. Hills likens the importance of place in fandom to that of organized religion, as both seem to benefit from an anchoring of rather amorphous conceptual material to an actual physical space.[20] To be sure, the fact that the Yankees are real on-field adversaries, forever anchored to their stadium and their city in the minds of Yankee haters, adds considerable heft to the enterprise, while allowing those haters to achieve a more nimble melding of the real and the imagined within the alternative habitus of Yankee hatred.

Interestingly, the project of creating an imagined alternative habitus housing the Yankee hater's negative conception of New York City is precisely what enables the Yankees' prominence as a globally recognized superteam. Of course, the imagined content in the alternative habitus fashioned by this global constituency is, unlike much of the reality of American influence abroad, relentlessly positive: a New York City that is representative of an amalgam of American affluence and influence, the benefits of which can best be accessed from an insider's position. Because such a position is unlikely for all but the few who succeed in making America their physical habitus, an alternative habitus that includes Yankee fandom must suffice. Of course, those baseball fans in the American heartland, dwarfed by the cultural shadow of New York City, tell a far different story of an arrogant, domineering city full of arrogant, domineering fans doing everything it can to crush the goodness of their hometown Heimat. So extensive is this sentiment west of the Hudson that a different sort of universal constituency seems to have formed among the baseball fans of North America: a Yankee hater fanbase, united by a rare loathing that can transcend the gulf created by individual team loyalties.

A good starting point for comprehending this secondary fanbase of Yankee hatred is the view of fandom offered by Fiske, which was briefly mentioned in the first chapter of this book. Claiming that the pleasure of fandom can be found through subversive readings of the fan objects offered up by the popular culture industry, Fiske's paradigm certainly provides a means for interpreting the activities of those who espouse contempt for Major League Baseball's most prominent fan object. Yet, this approach leaves some questions unanswered. For example, it does not fully explain why those same Yankee-hating fans would not also develop subversive readings of the prefabricated mythologies that are so central to the mainstream marketing of their own teams. Why do these equally hegemonic texts of the popular culture industry get a pass from these disempowered fans simply because they contain a hometown focus? Perhaps in the current age of highly advanced marketing, advertising, and audience measurement techniques, it's simply becoming too difficult for the bulk of fans to determine the difference between their truly oppositional fan text readings and one of the many intentionally edgy, pseudo-subversive fan objects sold as a means of short-circuiting meaningful fan activity. In addition, whether they accept a corporate vision of subversion or develop their own alternative reading of the standard company line, fans are still engaged in buying the objects of fandom that are being sold to them, which can only strengthen the position of those in power. To get past these issues, it may be necessary to view fans as something other than a monolithic consuming public. Nicholas Abercrombie and Brian Longhurst suggest a categorization of fandom based on differences in media utilization, fan interaction, and the specificity of fan objects.[21] The largest grouping, simply referred to as *fans*, displays a strong interest in the mediated presentation of a fan object, while avoiding any organized fan activity. *Cultists* display a more specialized interest in their objects of fandom, as well as in developing linkages to others with similar interest levels in the same fan object. But *enthusiasts* transcend the typical limitations of mass-mediated fandom by shifting the focus to the production of their own fan objects. While most followers of the game of baseball could be classified as casual fans or more committed cultists, those who identify themselves as Yankee haters might approach the status of the enthusiast. True, Yankee hatred is fashioned from select remnants of what might be considered the official Yankee fan text, unlike the made-from-scratch fan production that characterizes pure enthusiasts. But it's not as if there is a mainstream media programming genre for Yankee hatred; it is the responsibility of those who claim to be Yankee haters to actively construct the content of that particular fandom, and the vigor with which they do so is plainly evident in their message board discussions.

So, if we can view this fanbase of Yankee hatred as a collection of enthusiasts involved in the active construction of a non-official fan text, what might account for the specific nature of that fan text's content, and why might that content display some degree of variance among the specific team fanbases of Major League Baseball? Why would fans of, say, the Detroit Tigers and the Kansas City Royals end up hating the *same* Yankees for somewhat *different* reasons? Sandvoss makes an observation that gets us moving toward an answer to these questions when he cautions against assuming that any given fan text is either *open* or *closed*; that is, available either as raw material for alternative readings, or completely unavailable for this activity due to an absolute fixity of meaning. In place of this false either/or dichotomy, Sandvoss makes the claim that all texts are *polysemic*, bearing "a multiplicity of possible interpretations which are consciously realized by the reader."[22] Of course, it stands to reason that some fan texts will offer more interpretive possibilities than others, and that a fan may be free to simply adopt a preformed interpretation structured by the text's official creator or devise one of her own. But Sandvoss suggests that it is the quantity of interpretive possibilities within a text that determines the likelihood of truly alternate readings in which fans project qualities of the self onto the object of fandom:

> Only if fan texts function as a mirror, can fans find their reflected image in the object of fandom. Having stated that all texts are polysemic, because they cannot carry a single, definitive meaning, this supposes that at the end of the spectrum polysemic texts allow for so many different readings that they can no longer be meaningfully described as polysemic. The notion of self-reflection in fandom suggests that some texts come to function as a blank screen on which fans' self-image is reflected. These texts are *poly*-semic to a degree that they become *neutro*semic—in other words, carry no inherent meaning. By "neutrosemy" I describe the semiotic condition in which a text allows for so many divergent readings that, intersubjectively, it does not have any meaning at all.[23]

Could Yankee hatred constitute such a neutrosemic fan text, constructed differently by each hometown fanbase as a reflection of its particular local cultural ethos? This would account for the variations on the theme of Yankee hatred that exist across specific team fanbases. The fact that the official fan text of the Yankees is a rather distant object for fans in Detroit and Kansas City can only enhance its neutrosemic qualities, intensifying the need for those distant fans to construct various meanings that represent their localized opposition to the Yankees and the cultural ethos of New York City. After all, it's not as if the official Yankee fan text, the most revered and powerful fan text in the game, would deign to negotiate a mutually acceptable status with the other fan texts of Major League Baseball. Sandvoss acknowledges this distance factor as something that facilitates the development of neutrosemy and alternative readings:

> In contrast to forms of mediated interaction such as telephone calls or letters, the intimacy created in mediated quasi-interaction is non-reciprocal. While the fan interacts intensely with a particular text, the text does not talk

back . . . The greater the communicative distance, then, the lesser the text's denotative power and the greater the number of possible interpretations.[24]

Thus, 29 distinct versions of why baseball fans should hate the Yankees were developed, featuring a degree of overlapping self-reflection sufficient to provide otherwise antagonistic fans of competing teams a chance to find common cause. By reworking the preferred narrative of the glories of Yankeedom into one of resentment and loathing, this fanbase of Yankee haters might be seen as an insurgency against "America's Team" and the one-dimensional fan that Major League Baseball would surely welcome as an easily managed component of its business model. It should also be noted that within any team's fanbase, the number of Yankee-hater enthusiasts with the time and inclination to engage in this sort of fan text production would be rather small—too small, and too preoccupied with Yankee hatred, to provide a critical mass for encouraging subversive readings of the home-team fan text that could threaten the preservation of that local cultural ethos against which Yankee hatred is constructed. Therefore, each home team fan text, along with the identity of the fanbase, is preserved, while that small number of enthusiasts in each fanbase is free to extend its fandom into the secondary realm of Yankee hatred.

Of course, despite all this talk of cultural warfare between New York elitism and the humble authenticity of Middle America, one can be forgiven for wondering just how different followers of the Yankees could be from all those other fans across the country. After all, aren't we all just baseball fans, united in our love for the game, regardless of our affiliation with a particular team? Aren't we all Americans, united by a national ethos that transcends regional difference? Really, isn't that what the Civil War was all about? Well, perhaps Freud's discussion of his concept of *the narcissism of minor differences* could shed some light on these questions:

> Every time two families become connected by a marriage, each of them thinks itself superior to or of better birth than the other. Of two neighbouring towns each is the other's most jealous rival; every little canton looks down upon the others with contempt.[25]

We may all be Americans. We may all be baseball fans. But it's wise to remember that fandom is, as Bourdieu would term it, a project of distinction. If it weren't for small differences, how would we precisely define our projects of fandom? As alluded to earlier, this need for small differences can be extended to *imagined* differences projected onto that excluded other, just as an imagined other might be constructed *within* a fanbase. While Yankee haters seem somewhat willing to tolerate the many competing local versions of their secondary fan project, maybe the Yankees and other aspects of New York culture are just too different from the rest of baseball-loving America to be accommodated. Or perhaps these imperious East Coast entities are just too culturally close for comfort, a condition of being first among cultural equals that New Yorkers are all too willing to embrace. In any case, the goal is the legitimation of the fanbase through distinction and for that purpose, cultural closeness can be just as useful as cultural distance. But judging from the message board comments from Yankee haters, cultural distance stands as the greater motivation.

In the end, figuring out what Yankee hatred is really about involves viewing the development of the phenomenon at several different levels, with each subsequent level displaying a higher degree of social organization and relying on prior levels as a foundation. At the level of the individual fan, we find a psychological basis for Yankee hatred as an enjoyable adjunct to the positive association one develops with a home team. As a fan's need for a secondary source of enjoyment tends to increase whenever that home team fails to deliver the thrill of victory on a consistent basis, the reality of competition requiring that "some gotta win and some gotta lose" virtually ensures that at any given time, half of all baseball fans will be feeling this need. When these individual fans can find a common focus that allows for an overlapping of their psychological condition with that of others, internal states of mind can take on a social dimension. It's difficult to imagine a more ideal common focus for this process among American baseball fans than the New York Yankees, a team that is, arguably, more successful than any fan's home team, globally recognized as an iconic institution of the game and America itself, and representative of a New York City culture that represents an arrogant irritant to the cultural self-esteem of virtually every non-New Yorker in America. Add to this mythic complex of factors the fact that the Yankees are an actual on-field adversary for at least half the teams in Major League Baseball and the Yankees' folk-devil status becomes something very real in the immediate experience of baseball fans, transcending historical legend and serving as an active generator of ongoing animus. Given this dynamic, it's little wonder that the fanbase of every one of those other 29 Major League Baseball teams has developed some body of evidence that Yankee hatred is alive and well within its ranks. It's also clear that perhaps no other sentiment in baseball possesses the ability to coax fans out of their parochial allegiances and into a secondary fanbase uniting the entirety of baseball fandom. When you think about it, facilitating this kind of unity among what are normally antagonistic, fiercely competitive fanbases is something that only the Yankees could achieve. Perhaps it's something they should be as proud of as their 26 World Series championships.

But what of the future of Yankee hatred? Will the post-9/11 proclamation that "We're all New Yorkers now" finally come to fruition through some sort of delayed reaction, forcing all baseball fans to become shareholders in the Yankee fan experience? Or will the hatred thrive indefinitely, even if the Yankees become impotent patsies and fail to add a 27th World Series trophy to their display case? Well, let's consider that as these words are being written, the display case and those 26 trophies are being carefully packed up and moved to "The House Next Door To the House That Ruth Built": the new Yankee Stadium. After allowing for several adjustments to the estimated cost, it appears that this new baseball cathedral will end up with a price tag of about $1.6 billion, excluding the several hundred million dollars that the taxpayers of New York City will throw toward the infrastructure improvements necessitated by the project.[26] Interestingly, this expenditure will result in fewer Yankee fans being able to see their team in action on any given day, as the new stadium shaves off more than 4,000 seats from the capacity of the original Yankee Stadium. However, those new seats are wider, and they do have cup holders. In terms of other improvements on the original, consider the following: 56 private luxury suites, up from 19; 410 party suites, compared to none next door; 1 concession stand for every 172 fans, versus the 1 for every 260 fans from a thinner time in history; 11,560 square feet of retail team store space, up from a mere 6,800; 14 dining and lounge options, including a sports bar, steakhouse, and martini bar, compared to a paltry 4 options in the original model; and, to ensure that all those calories go home with you, the number of elevators has been increased from 3 to 16.[27] Of course, enjoying all of those amenities will cost you. While bleacher seats can be obtained for the same $12 price of the old Yankee Stadium, it seems the definition of the term "bleacher seat" has been somewhat restricted. Now, some of those seats beyond the outfield wall carry a ticket price of $100. As for those front-row seats right behind home plate that the bleacher bums can only dream about, they now qualify as a significant dream upgrade at $2,500 per seat. Lonn Trost, the team's chief operating officer, has tried to drown out the sound of all those fans' jaws hitting the floor by framing the new stadium's seat pricing as something of a Robin Hood scenario, explaining that "we recognize everybody can't afford the suites. At the same time, we're trying to allow those suite prices to subsidize the other seating in the stadium."[28] Sean Pate, head of corporate communications for StubHub, the official fan-to-fan ticket marketplace of the Yankees, offered somewhat colder comfort to the average fan, observing that "Joe Lunchbox never considered buying those tickets when they cost $1,000 in the current [old] stadium, let alone $2,500 at the new one."[29] But remember the upside: all of the seats, regardless of price, now have cup holders.

While spokespeople might prefer to justify such extravagance in terms of providing a first-class fan experience for first-class fans, it's difficult to ignore the importance of the new Yankee Stadium as a central component in maintaining the organization's position as the most financially blessed franchise in Major League Baseball. By upgrading to a state-of-the-art stadium, the Yankees organization can now justify the increases in ticket and luxury suite license prices, which will result in a greatly enhanced revenue stream for what was already the wealthiest team in baseball. Ample evidence of the rich getting richer accumulated well before the new stadium's 2009 grand opening. On November 13, 2008, the Yankees acquired Nick Swisher in a trade with the Chicago White Sox in an effort to fill the hole left at first base by the departure of Jason Giambi. Despite having the worst batting average of any player with enough plate appearances to qualify for the 2008 batting title, the Yankees saw fit to take on Swisher and the final three years of a contract that will pay him more than $21 million.[30] Next, in December, the Yankees reached contract agreements with two highly coveted free agent pitchers: former Milwaukee Brewer C. C. Sabathia, who received a seven-year deal worth $161 million, and former Toronto Blue Jay A. J. Burnett, who signed for five years and $82.5 million.[31] Then, upon realizing that they'd be paying the worst full-time hitter in baseball more than $21 million to be their first baseman for the next three years, the Yankees decided that they'd remedy the problem in classic Yankee fashion. On December 23, 2008, they reached an agreement with prized free agent first baseman Mark Teixeira on an eight-year contract worth $180 million.[32] After giving themselves this little Christmas gift, the Yankees were positioned to enter the 2009 season with not only the four highest-paid players in baseball, but with a total payroll that was actually less than their record-setting $222.5 million payroll of 2008. News of this newfound austerity must have come as a relief to Yankee spokespeople, who were tasked with addressing the receipt of a $26.9 million Major League Baseball luxury tax bill generated by that 2008 payroll just one day before the Teixeira deal was announced.[33] Of course, entering into these four contracts worth in excess of $444 million can only serve to make Yankee fans salivate uncontrollably at the prospect of cheering on a team positioned for postseason dominance for years to come. It should also make those higher ticket prices at the new Yankee Stadium a bit easier to swallow, which, in turn, will ensure an even greater revenue stream in the future. Indeed, it seems the rich really do get richer.

Meanwhile, the small-market Milwaukee Brewers, who were never really in a position to retain the services of Sabathia and were counting on receiving a first-round draft choice as compensation for his departure, faced the prospect of being even poorer than expected. It turns out that Teixeira was ranked higher than Sabathia in the Elias player rankings, the system used to determine the draft pick a team must surrender as compensation for signing a free agent. Because the Yankees were in the unique financial position to sign both Teixeira and Sabathia, Teixeira's former team, the relatively affluent Angels, received the Yankees' first-round pick in the 2009 player draft. Had Teixeira been signed by any of the other four teams making a serious bid for his services, the Brewers would have received the high draft pick that is so crucial to the small-market strategy of rebuilding from within. But the Angels, Orioles, Nationals, and Red Sox all failed in their attempts to compete with Yankee dollars. So, the Brewers must be content with receiving the Yankees' second-round pick in compensation for losing a player considered by many to be the best southpaw in the game. Doug Melvin, the Brewers' general manager, reacted to this development with a mixture of resignation and disappointment, which surely must be a common attitudinal complex in many small-market front offices:

> The Angels had a better record than us and the Blue Jays, and the Brewers and the Blue Jays got shoved down the food chain . . . We have dropped forty-six slots in the 2009 draft, and we will be dropping even more because there are so many compensation picks. The second round will be almost the third round, in the way that it will develop.[34]

Still, some small-market team executives, perhaps resigned to the fact that they'll never be able to compete with the Yankees' checkbook, maintain that this Yankee hegemony is good for the game of baseball. After all, none of these small-market executives are refusing to cash those annual luxury tax checks. Then again, nothing says that cash-strapped teams struggling to keep the lights on must use that money to acquire players that might deliver a championship. But superclubs like the Yankees generate fan interest, they argue, and this heightened interest generates increased attendance and increased revenues whenever they play a small-market team in a small-market stadium. Of course, this trickle-down argument parallels the standard defense offered by advocates of unrestricted free market capitalism which, in the process of generating impressive amounts of systemic wealth, often produces indispensible individual participants that are simply "too big to fail." But as players reported to spring training in 2009 amid a global economic meltdown, which many observers trace to the excesses committed by financial players who were too big to fail, perhaps even this defense of Yankee dominance will lose some of its luster. So, again, what does all of this mean for the future of Yankee hatred?

Rest easy, folks. The future seems secure.

Epilogue

YANKEE LOVE AND THE NEW YANKEE STADIUM

Despite all the flattering talk emanating from team spokespeople about providing a first-class fan experience for first-class fans, it's difficult to think of the main motive for building a new Yankee Stadium as anything other than a desire to enhance an already prodigious Yankee revenue stream. Of course, generating gobs of cash and privileging the fan base are certainly not mutually exclusive goals for any baseball franchise. Shiny new stadiums enhance revenues, enhanced revenues attract better players, better players increase the likelihood of a winning team, and a winning team is arguably the most crucial component of any first-class fan experience. But the obvious symbiosis contained in this formula might not be front and center in the consciousness of the average fan looking forward to spending a day at the ballpark.

More likely, he's concerned with more immediate issues. Did he remember the tickets? Since we might be talking about some sort of "e-ticket," does the printer on his home computer provide the resolution required to print something that will be properly scanned at the turnstile? Did he remember his ATM card in case Junior wants a second nine-dollar hot dog in addition to that sack full of team merchandise? Did Junior remember to pee before everyone raced out of the house? Such is the difference in mindset between those who show up at the ballpark to watch and those who show up to work. Those in the latter category who work for the Yankees have been wildly successful at managing this formula for success, maintaining a gushing revenue stream, building an enormous and dedicated fanbase, and inspiring legions of Yankee haters in the process. Throughout this book, we've heard from many of those Yankee haters, virtually all of whom claim a primary allegiance to one of the other 29 teams of Major League Baseball. But, except for the occasional defensive response to a Yankee hater's invective, we haven't heard much from members of that enormous and dedicated Yankee fanbase. Is the fan experience for these folks just all peaches and cream? If not, what objects have they singled out as a focus for their negativity? Finally, more to the point of this epilogue, who better to assess the new Yankee Stadium than those fans who possess an encyclopedic knowledge of the original?

The importance of physical place in the lives of sports fans was briefly addressed earlier in this book, with the focus often being on the stadium as a type of sacred space dedicated to the reimagining and preservation of the concept of a comfortable and permanent home in an increasingly mobile and rootless society. Many are the tales of the dedicated fan who simply must sit in the same stadium seat whenever he attends a game, or whose soul will not rest peacefully unless his ashes are scattered over the field of play shared by his team. But the regular-season opening of the new Yankee Stadium on April 16, 2009, provides a valuable laboratory for examining just how strongly issues of material culture factor into the construction of fandom. Of course, we're talking about a stadium burdened with the task of replacing the original Yankee Stadium, which sets an impossibly high bar in terms of meeting the fans' expectations; the history of the effort to build that replacement reflects the difficulty of clearing that bar.

Thoughts of a new address for the Yankees date back at least to the 1980s, when George Steinbrenner contemplated moving his team to some other neighborhood considered safer than the South Bronx.[1] But as the 1990s wore on, the economy improved, the Yankees played better, attendance went up, and the Bronx didn't look so nasty anymore. Still, as other teams moved into new stadiums that generated deeper revenue streams, dreams of a new stadium in the Bronx refused to die. Enter Mayor Rudy Giuliani who, in 1998, thought it might be a better idea if the Yankees moved to a new ballpark on Manhattan's West Side, until he decided that an even better idea for that location would be a retractable-dome football stadium for the New York Jets, accompanied by a new and improved version of Madison Square Garden.[2] So, it was back to the Bronx for the Yankees, as Giuliani proposed that the city fund the construction of a new Yankee Stadium there.[3] But mayors come and go, and as Mayor Michael Bloomberg replaced Giuliani, plans for that new Yankee Stadium in the Bronx were seen as a bit too extravagant for a post-9/11 New York, in addition to being a financial crimp on Bloomberg's desire to complete that West Side stadium as a crucial part of his bid to bring the 2012 Olympic Games to the city.[4] So, Bloomberg put the brakes on the Giuliani plan for a new Yankee

Stadium in the Bronx, only to resurrect the idea in 2005, after the West Side stadium plan died in the state legislature. As it turned out, the announcement of a deal for a new stadium for the Mets, which could also be used for the 2012 Olympics, followed news of the demise of the West Side project by a mere eight days. Perhaps fearing that good news for the Mets might result in the long-threatened departure of the Yankees from New York, a deal for a new Yankee Stadium in the Bronx was announced three days later.[5]

Of course, this complex tale has everything to do with political ambition and financial machinations, and very little to do with Yankee fans. Regardless of the details, how would they react to any plan that would evict them from the House That Ruth Built? While the notion that Yankee fans view themselves as somehow exceptional tends to enrage legions of non-Yankee fans, even the most diehard Yankee hater might have to admit that, when it comes to Yankee Stadium, they may have a point. As a Cleveland Indians fan, I can recall meeting the opening of Jacobs Field in 1994 with a massive sigh of relief. At last, the Tribe and I would be forever liberated from that horrid "mistake on the lake" that was Cleveland Municipal Stadium. Sure, that place is a big part of my personal history as a baseball fan. But I'm quite happy just to keep the memories and ditch the structure. I get the feeling that most fans of teams that move into new stadiums feel much the same way. After a bit of initial ambivalence, there's nothing like a fresh start in a spanking new ballpark to rekindle dreams of a pennant. But it has to be different for Yankee fans. After all, they've seen their team accumulate 39 American League pennants, and all but the first 2 were won in Yankee Stadium. In other words, Yankee fans are not exactly in need of a fresh start, and Ryanation4 seems to concur in his response to a fellow Yankee fan's hopeful post regarding the eventual acceptance of the new Yankee Stadium:

> [Ncyankfan7 writes] I find it kind of funny that media types gushed over new ballparks like Camden Yards, Jacobs Field, Coors Field, etc. They said they were beautiful and state of the art. Now the Yankees have a new stadium and everybody longs for the old park. I fully understand the tradition (saw my first game in 1960) but change and something new is not bad. It takes time for any stadium to have its own memories, and the minute the Yankees win their first championship in this park I think people's attitudes will be different.[6]
>
> [Ryanation4 replies] A few things wrong here. First of all, yes, Camden, Jacobs Field, Coors Field, PNC Park, etc. were praised for being such wonderful new stadiums. The problem: what history did the O's, Indians, Rockies, and Pirates have in old stadiums? I mean some memories here and there, for sure. But NOTHING comparing to the history of Yankee Stadium

(I refuse to call the new stadium Yankee Stadium because it's nowhere near close.) The new stadium plays differently, looks different, and has no aura or mystique factor. There's no WOW of a new player walking into the new stadium. The draw for young guys used to be, "Wow . . . I'm stepping where Babe Ruth, Mickey Mantle, Ted Williams, Lou Gehrig, etc., have patrolled the field. I'm stepping where history has been made." Now, there's no grand feeling walking into the new stadium. Just another stadium.[7]

For Ryaation4 and those who share his view, Yankee fans may be in a singular, exceptional position among baseball fans of needing to preserve as much of the past as possible. And for them, that past is inextricably linked to a precise physical location. Not only must any new stadium achieve the impossible task of looking exactly the same as the original, it must somehow possess the same intangible atmosphere that resulted in 26 World Series titles. Even the slightest deviation from its predecessor would surely be blamed for any failure to win a 27th. As absurd as it may sound, any *new* Yankee Stadium would be found lacking unless it were the *old* Yankee Stadium. Or maybe not. Shoveit6963 contends that attempting to replicate a past as glorious as that of the original Yankee Stadium is simply futile, and that fully embracing the choice, once made, to create something completely different would be the only way to properly preserve that past:

> First of all, my house is over 100 years old but doesn't completely resemble its former self. But with that said, it's still my home, even with the renovations. You can knock it down, and build it across the street, even have it more true to its original form but with increased technology and added amenities, but that doesn't mean that it's going to feel like home. I'd rather just buy a whole new house altogether. If they weren't ready to abandon the old concept and start from scratch, then they shouldn't have moved out of the stadium in the first place. I'm not sure that'd ever happen, to outgrow the tradition, but so be it! The Yankees of today are regarded as a free spending empire, but they were always sort of grounded by the rich tradition of the old stadium. Even many Yankee haters respected the stadium and what it stood for. It wasn't the most accommodating stadium, it lacked many basic amenities, but it was still beautiful nonetheless, and people still came in droves to see it. Now, we have a ballpark that fits our reputation of being frivolous and over the top. It's just a mallpark in my eyes.[8]

Sorry guys, but not only did the front office think the old stadium needed to be scrapped, they thought it needed to be cloned. A genetically modified clone with lots of bells and whistles, that is. But, judging from the early buzz among Yankee fans, many of them simply aren't ready for that brave new world.

Perhaps it's to be expected that any early rumblings regarding the new Yankee Stadium would be somewhat negative. After all, reaction to anything new seems to skew negative simply because those who are content with the change have nothing to complain about. Still, a significant number of Yankee fans felt the need to register their approval despite an opening day loss to the Cleveland Indians:

> The NY Yankees always do it right and today was just another example of why this franchise stands out above ALL others in ALL sports. Nobody matches the Yankees and for all who hate them I can only feel pity for never knowing how good greatness can be.[9]

Of course, this celebratory post from Stevem7 manages to convey all the exceptionalism and superiority that Yankee haters assume to be at the core of every Yankee fan. But some, like WoodyDee, would replace such assertiveness and swagger with a more maudlin version of positivity:

> I'm not sure if anyone has mentioned how ultimately fitting it was to see [Yankee catcher] Jorge [Posada's] home run, the first ever home run hit in the new stadium, land at the feet of the immortals, alone without anyone there in Monument Park. If you take one thing away from today's game, see that as a positive sign of good things to come. Respect to the traditions and remembering our past. Yankee Stadium becomes Heritage Field—I saw that sign posted on the old stadium wall. The last thing I did walking away from the game today, I stopped at the River Avenue side of the stadium near the old bleacher entrance and kissed the building, then said "Thank You" and walked away.[10]

One can almost hear the eyes of all those Yankee haters rolling in unison. Still, most fans can probably forgive WoodyDee's sentimentality, especially in the aftermath of an opening day loss. But as the second game of the inaugural series resulted in a victory for the Yankees, it also provided an opportunity for Yankee fans to get a bit more specific in their assessment of the new Yankee Stadium. After offering some general praise for the stadium's amenities, PridePowerPinstripes posted a rather extensive list of pros and cons, with the latter category including a brief comment about his seat facing center field rather than having the home plate angle he had been told was a feature of the new stadium's design. Among the many responses to his post were several that echoed his very positive reaction, but that seating issue seemed to touch a raw nerve among the Yankee faithful:

> [MarisHOF writes:] The main "obstructed" seats (which I didn't see for myself, because I just couldn't get there) are in the bleachers, alongside the

centerfield restaurant which prevents a view of the outfield on the opposite side from where you're sitting. With all due respect to the Yanks, that suk-kkks—and no matter how loud we say it, it won't be loud enough. About the supposed "angle" of the seats—YOU'RE RIGHT. They were supposed to be angled, but they aren't really . . . I made a point of checking this on Thursday . . . Cliff's Notes: the "angling" is disappointing, because it's not very much. Unless you're near home plate or in HR territory, you have to turn your head or sit crooked most of the time.[11]

[PridePowerPinstripes replies] I tried all I could to get into the Field Level, like where the leather seats are. I asked one of the guys with the "How may I help you?" signs and he said that the lower down to the field you go, the more angled your seats will be. I guess you have to pay more for your seat to be angled.:-) It doesn't bother me much, though. My neck was a little stiff after yesterday, but it was before the game, too . . . Overall, the stadium is just an absolute palace![12]

[MarisHOF replies] One other thing we should emphasize—and IMO it's not so good. In the past, you could walk into any section you wanted (except for the very front area on field level), just to take a look if you felt like it. And later in the game, you could go and sit in a different section if there were empty seats. You can't do that now, except to move elsewhere within your own section. At least not easily. Unless you talk a good game. :-) And even then. I was able to sweet-talk the ushers into letting me do a BRIEF check of seats in other sections, and maybe it was mainly because I was able to show that my "actual" seats were "better" than where I wanted to go. I'm not sure they would have let me do it otherwise. And they made me feel like a trespasser, and like they were doing me a favor, which I guess they sort of were.[13]

[Okefanokie replies] They can't be any less angled than the ones in the old stadium, LOL. I haven't been there yet but I am not even thinking about that. Even though my tickets used to be right behind home plate so the neck twist wasn't something to worry about. Now, as you know, I am in the ex-tended infield so I am sure I will have to turn. I might decide to angle my entire body and sacrifice back pain for a painless neck, LOL.[14]

Is there a chiropractor in the house? Based on this exchange, maybe man-agement should have included therapeutic massage among the new Yankee Stadium's amenity upgrades. Sure, Yankee fans have come to expect the best. But this sort of critique offered up on Day Two of the new Yankee Sta-dium seems downright persnickety. As stated earlier, several very positive comments were also posted to this thread. But Roywitefan was more than willing to douse those glimmers of hope:

Glad you guys like it. To me, it's just a big mall with a baseball field inside. No real character or charm. And it's just so gaudy and over the top. Sure, the frieze is nice, as is the exterior façade. But aside from that, there's not much to make you remember "original" Yankee Stadium. I hope I will grow to like it over time, but I doubt it.[15]

One of the most frequent points of discussion among Yankee fans regarding the new stadium focused on its physical differences from the original, with those differences often portrayed as deficiencies. Yet, despite the prevalence of complaints about architectural shortcomings, many Yankee fans felt compelled to defend their team's new confines. This exchange regarding the aforementioned seating and sightline issue typifies that give and take:

[Portwa writes] Anyone at the game yesterday sitting in the left or right field area—could you see the entire outfield from your seats? I've heard [new Yankee Stadium architectural firm] HOK parks can cut out outfield corners in their designs.[16]

[46fan4evr replies] I was in left field bleachers section 238 and could see the whole field—in section 239 you can't see right field at all unless you are in the first couple of rows, and the same would happen with left field if you're in section 201 in right field. They do have three TV screens mounted on the wall of the restaurant so that you can see that way, but you can't see the actual field.[17]

[RayG replies] I think those corner cutoffs are almost the same as the OYS [old Yankee Stadium]. From my seats in [section] 413, you lose the extreme right field corner—EXACTLY the same as my seats in section 17 in OYS. Maybe a little less of a cutoff, but I think the viewing experience will be pretty much the same.[18]

[Ruhikuz replies] Those people who are cut off are also only paying $5 a game—a bargain, IMO—only because you can now walk anywhere you want in the stadium with a bleacher seat. I would buy a couple of those $5 seats for life if they became available.[19]

[46fan4evr replies] Yup, $5 is a great price.[20]

Portwa's rather objective inquiry about seats with obstructed sightlines not only generated a confirmation but also several replies that come rather close to justifying such seating based on its replication of the same deficiency in the original Yankee Stadium and its cost effectiveness compared to seats from which a fan might actually see the entire field. Indeed, some fans' insistence on exact replication of the original Yankee Stadium includes some of the very things they probably used to enjoy complaining about.

A similar conversational dynamic developed in reference to the inordinate number of home runs hit during the new Yankee Stadium's inaugural series:

[84yrs4_26 writes] Wondering what you guys think of the twenty dingers already hit at Yankee Stadium. I'm a little fearful of what this could mean for all the pitching help we got this year and if, at least for home games, it could negate it. It's like a wind tunnel between the old and new Yankee Stadium, and keep in mind many are saying that wind blows from home plate to the outfield (per Peter Gammons) due to the open-face concourse. How could engineers not keep something so simple in mind?[21]

[Riron replies] IMO, the biggest factor is that the climate has been extremely dry in the Northeast—like 14% humidity. That is Southwest dryness. With that the ball is much lighter and more lively . . . The old stadium had a depressed playing field. I assume the new one is not (that can also contribute to the high numbers). I think the HR production will drop as the humidity increases.[22]

[Stevem7 replies] So far, there haven't been any night games in the regular season to tell if the wind is going to be less at night. I think we need to get eight or ten night games under our belts before making a decision. Additionally, [Yankees' General Manager Brian] Cashman pointed out that when the old stadium is knocked down it will change the wind pattern off the river. And finally, YES pointed out in their broadcast that the outer wall of the stadium in right field is open where it never was in the old Yankee Stadium. So, possibly, that is a tweak that they might have to do to close in the outer wall of the building.[23]

[Babebomber replies] I just read an article that said the strong westerly winds which are typical in spring and later fall are in part responsible for the home run derby. The article claims the home runs should be less once summer comes. We'll see.[24]

[62 nova replies] Give it a rest. The Yankee offense will benefit from the way the ball flies out of there, too. I don't understand what the problem is in your mind. As long as both teams play in the same conditions, who cares?[25]

Citing factors such as time of day, time of season, surrounding structures, and correctable design flaws as contributors to inordinately high home run totals at the new Yankee Stadium seems reasonable. And 62 nova makes a good point in reminding us all that both the Yankees and their adversaries will be playing on the same field under equivalent conditions that will favor neither. But, Riron—desert-like humidity prevailing in the Northeast?— I'm no meteorologist, but this seems like a defensive stretch that only a Yankee fan harboring some doubts about the new ballpark could muster.

Beyond the seemingly trivial complaints about things like protective netting diminishing what used to be the superior clarity of televised images in the old Yankee Stadium, fastidious Yankee fans in need of exact replication of the past seem somewhat suspicious of claims that the new stadium provides an exact replication of the original stadium's playing field. The following exchange regarding the supposedly exact duplication of the outfield fence is but one example:

[9roger9 writes] They may be the same distances that were on the walls in the old stadium, but it looks to me like the angles and curvature of the walls in the new stadium are totally different. By reducing the curvature of the wall, I think that maybe they have shortened the porches in both left and right . . . What do you think?[26]

[RayG replies] I read that as well. While the numbers at the signs reflect the distances, the walls have been flattened to reduce the curve. Probably to make it easier for seat placement.[27]

[Joiseyank replies] I was at the game yesterday, Sunday 4/19, and sat in the main level in foul territory before the left field foul pole, section 231. I agree that the dimensions are NOT the same. If you sit out near the foul poles and take a walk toward the outfield fences from above you can clearly see that there are sections of the outfield fence that are not curved but run in straight lines unlike the old stadium where the entire outfield wall was curved. The best example would be to go to the main level concourse (now really the second level above the premium seats) and walk to the end just before the stairs to go down to the bleachers and bleacher food courts. If you look down at the outfield fences from that vantage point you can see very clearly, for instance, that there is no curve in the wall whatsoever from one side of the Yankee bullpen to the other. It is a straight line and if so, the fence must be shorter there than in the old stadium where it was curved in that area. Same for the visitor's bullpen. Whether other sections of the outfield fence are straight or curved I couldn't tell from that view, but clearly the bullpen wall has no curve whatsoever in it.[28]

[MarisHOF replies] I'm quite sure the "curvatures" are different, which means not all distances are the same as before. But I think it's likely that the "main" distances—i.e. the marked ones—are the same.[29]

[Sparkylyle replies] Actually, the distance difference in RF is very different; 5–10 feet. On other sites guys have taken aerial shots and blueprints and overlayed them to show just how much shorter RF is. Yes, they put in the 385' and the 399' [signs], but they are not in the same location (power alley) as OYS. They are much closer to CF.[30]

While this kind of sweating of the technical details seems not only harmless but ultimately solvable through verification, a more troubling schism developed when a discussion about the decibel levels in each stadium quickly evolved into rumblings of class warfare:

[A-roddaman writes] It is dead silent. This is what happens when the idiots outprice the real fans in favor of the snobby, rich fools who wear a f****** dress shirt and tie to a game.[31]

[Close2thebats replies] It's also due to the shape and slope of the grandstand. Regardless of all the BS they spew about more fans being closer to the field, that's entirely untrue.[32]

[Pdxyankee1 replies] The upper deck at the old stadium felt like it was literally on top of the field. To opposing pitchers, it must have felt like the fans were very close to them. That could rattle a pitcher. We will no longer enjoy this advantage at the new park.[33]

[A-roddaman replies] Look at all the empty seats. Nobody in their right mind is going to pay $2500 for a seat.[34]

[A-roddaman adds] Yup. Watching the Old YS during playoff time gave ME the chills. Imagine how opposing pitchers felt. There was not an empty seat in the house and the real fans were there, screaming their heads off.[35]

[Danyeo replies] I agree with you on all points. These are not real fans buying up these seats. Just people who have money who want to be at the new park because it's a happening. The actual game is secondary to these snobs. I bet they're spending their time looking out for celebrities rather than the pitch count.[36]

[A-roddaman replies] Yup. It's sad, really.[37]

No strangers to the concept of cause and effect, Yankee fans in another discussion thread were easily connecting the dots represented by sonic deficiency, empty seats, and the inflated price tag that keeps those seats empty and silent:

[96champs writes] I was there on Sunday, 4-19-09. The playing field looks exactly the same. A casual fan who has been to some games won't notice a lot of differences. It just doesn't have the same feel as the old place. S*cks that [stadium announcer] Bob Sheppard isn't doing the games. This bothered me more than anything. Now they have a guy with a boring voice on the PA. "Seats Between the Bases" were only about 50% full. They were moving people down to fill these seats with special "seating upgrade" announcements in between innings.[38]

[Scottwaz replies] Was there Saturday. Couldn't hear anything clear over the sound system, from upper deck to the concourse behind home plate. I went everywhere from the moment the gates opened until I deserted the place after four innings of boring embarrassment. Twenty-something announcer muffled. No character to his voice. Video screen audio with too much dynamics. Need a good compressor/limiter and an acoustic analyzer to EQ [equalize] the sound. Large PA speakers are needed on either side of the video wall. All music was soft to the ears. The old PA system was intimidating! And I loved that the wind moved the sound through the air that sometimes it was hard to hear. But it was loud! The outfield wall cushions are violet in the sun. Bring back the lighter blue. 1/3 of all the Queen's seats were empty. Far too much concrete showing. Nothing uglier than bare concrete. I'm afraid it's a "me-too" park . . . After three innings I left the upper deck and found myself on the concourse comfortably standing right behind home plate with a great $2500 view for $25. Bad move. The grandeur of old was that you had to get back to your seat to see the ball game. It was the beckoning, the siren that drew you to the field. With open views to the field, you remove the curtain from the man standing behind the curtain. The Wizard wasn't so grand anymore, was he? Should I mention $9 beers and obstructed bleacher seat views? Sad. It's a plastic mock-up of the old place. Way too neat. You couldn't put the facade across center field and raise the team flags so I knew what place everyone in the East was in? Exacting the dimensions and touting that as the crown jewel of your accomplishment is not enough![39]

[RIEHL221 replies] I was there Friday and Sunday (I know-lucky me). Anyway, the stadium is overwhelming and there is a lot to see. I have to agree with others in that it was much more quiet than the old stadium. I don't know if it has to do with there being less people there, or due to people walking around the stadium more just trying to see everything and not really paying attention to the game. Overall, I give the stadium an A, but I do miss the old stadium because it just seemed more electric. I am hoping that once everyone gets to know the new stadium, it will become loud again.[40]

[Scottwaz replies] I sincerely hope someone from the Yankees reads this! This is YANKEE STADIUM we are talking about here. The ballpark reeks of "expansion" team nouveau retro. And rich people don't clap and yell as loud as excited families of four once did. So, now I've got this and ten years of A-Fraud to live with. Egads. Thank goodness for MLB Network and all the classics they show. I can watch lots of old time footage. Scott Wasienko, 35 year fan, first game Shea Stadium 1975. My father is still embarrassed that he brought his son to Shea Stadium to see his first Yankees game. Saturday, I brought him to new Yankee Stadium and I was just as embarrassed. You call me and limo me up and I'll take you through the entire stadium with pad and pencil and tell you what needs fixin'! P.S.: the bathrooms are great. Good going.[41]

[Stevem7 replies] Wish we could get a poster or two that sits in those $2625 seats. I'd dearly love to hear someone/anyone explain to me how one ballgame is worth that much money. Game 7 of the World Series isn't worth that much.[42]

[161curse replies] I sat in the $2,500 seats. It was great. I paid $3 for an upper deck seat. I waited until about the fourth inning, [when] the people in the good seats start to leave. I wandered down from my $3 seat and was plotting where I should try to sit. I saw a great seat about 10 rows back from the Yankee dugout. I folded up a $10 bill and placed it under my ticket. I showed the redcoat ticket taker my upper deck ticket with the $10 bill sneaking out from under it so he could see it. He took the ticket with the tenner and escorted me to a great seat . . . Oh wait, that was 1974 or 1975. Sorry.[43]

Well, 96champs will be pleased to know that the absence of Bob Sheppard's non-boring voice was merely a temporary deficiency due to the announcer's recovery from a bronchial infection.[44] And many of the deficiencies cited by Scottwaz are remediable, including the pricing structure blamed for all those empty seats and absent decibels. But 161curse's recollection of a simpler, more authentic period in Yankee fan history will not be easily erased by any fan-friendly cost reductions in the future. After all, you can't unring a bell. And with their imposition of a comparatively immoderate price of admission, the Yankees have chimed in loud and clear regarding their desire for an increasingly upscale, financially privileged fanbase. Of course, the demands of being a committed soldier in this class struggle don't easily mesh with the demands of being a committed Yankee fan, and significant bandwidth was utilized by those fans in order to begin the task of reconciling those conflicting roles:

[Sgh07 writes] I haven't been to the stadium in years actually, because between ticket prices, gas and tolls, parking and beverages (sodas), it would cost me at least $100 for my daughter and myself. I just looked over the ticket prices and could not believe the costs. And the food menus are prohibitive. I think the Steinbrenners should rot in some third [world] country jail at the prices they are charging, even if it's not them directly. Baseball used to be for the fans, not the Bernie Madoffs of the society.[45]

[Nyygal007 replies] Well, that's good news for the rest of us. One less annoying whiner at the stadium. THANKS! And have a great day![46]

[Okefanokie replies] Glad you got that off your chest. In the meantime, my tickets are $20. Not sure if that warrants rotting in a third world jail.[47]

[Sgh07 replies] I guess you sat in nose bleed country. Anybody who supports this team has to have a neurologist examine them. The Steinbrenners have gotten away with murder . . . This hurts the little guy and, based on your $20 tickets, you're a little guy.[48]

[Okefanokie replies] I've been sitting in nosebleed country since the day of Munson and Nettles and I don't have a problem with it.[49]

[46fan4evr replies] Bleacher seats are $14 each and you can bring your own food/beverages. It's what I do. If you really want to go, you can find a way.[50]

[Ruhikuz replies] These people who complain about the cost of going to a game never intended to go to a game anyway. This guy is probably not even a Yankee fan. The vast majority of the upper deck is the same cost as it was. They say who wants to sit in nosebleed seats. Obviously, they have never sat upstairs because those seats are great.[51]

[Nyygal007 replies] They can't sit in the bleachers or the upper deck. They're entitled to the good seats, doncha know! I remember sitting in the very last row and just being happy to be there![52]

[HolyCanoli replies] Can't agree more. Any REAL fan of the GAME of baseball understands that the upper tier seats are the best seats in the house. There is NO DEBATE. It offers you the opportunity to see everything. All these cry babies that complain about the upper deck have no knowledge about anything.[53]

[46fan4evr replies] That's how I feel about it. I'm just happy to be there.[54]

[DJmuggs replies] First of all, nowadays, how far is $100 REALLY gonna get you anyway? Second, you're not watching the freakin' Jays, or Marlins, or some pathetic organization like that where the owners take 90% of the profits. You're stepping into a $1.6 BILLION stadium, with the top payroll team in all sports. If you can't afford a $100 day for you and your daughter to enjoy, then just don't go. We're not in the '90s anymore, pal. It costs money to have fun.[55]

It's difficult to believe that Sgh07's complaint about the high cost of things isn't drawn directly from the same middle-class hymnal of gripes routinely used by the others in this discussion. Yet, focusing that complaint on the new Yankee Stadium unleashed a torrent of criticism that casts Sgh07 as the consummate unappreciative cheapskate. Even his fandom for the Yankees and baseball itself is questioned by fans that seem to view the endurance of increasing financial hardship as some sort of loyalty test. Perhaps it was his harsh words about the Steinbrenners that inspired others to demand he just shut up, pay up, and break out the binoculars. But whatever the cause, the result is the classic divide-and-conquer dynamic that often accompanies class warfare: get members of the other class to argue amongst themselves, and the battle is half won. Still, not every online discussion about ticket prices resulted in a threat to class solidarity—even when a Red Sox fan got the ball rolling:

[Redsox17 writes] Keep up the "it's only money" or "it's not my money" talk. Ha! You helped buy A-Rod's gold-plated tanning bed and his Chapstick closet. But the Yanks can justify paying A-Rod $30 million a year when he's forty-two because they have suckers like you making excuses for $2,500 seats. The George Jr.'s are making a mockery of you. What an embarrassment. Brand new stadium and almost every seat around the base path was completely empty! I thought I was watching a game from the '80s. But at least you have a Hard Rock Cafe there. Just what every ballpark needs.[56]

[Ncyankfan7 replies] There is no excuse for $2500 seats and I am glad they are empty. I am sure the price is going to change next year because they will lose revenue if these seats remain empty.[57]

And not every Yankee fan succumbed to humorless defensiveness when an opening day combination of high prices, empty seats, and a Yankee loss rekindled fears of failure among the faithful:

[1927yankee writes] $2,500 to watch a blowout—unreal. Year after year, it's the same Yankees: .500 till all-star break, and then the "closed door team meetings," then all the "soul searching," and then they get you all excited, and BAM!!! They are eliminated from the first round of the playoffs. I keep reading, "it's just ten games," "season just started," etc. Frankly, I have been reading the same thing since 2004, and year after year its more money, higher ticket prices and falling way short of expectations.[58]

[Sc1yankee replies] Try to look at the bright side. At least it wasn't $3,500 for falling short of expectations. Now don't you feel better? You already saved a THOUSAND dollars!!![59]

Sc1yankee's good humor might be exactly what distraught Yankee fans need to adjust to their move across the street. Then again, his sniggering speculation seemed to expose yet another raw nerve in the fanbase when he dared to suggest that the move may have resulted in a new, inverted Curse of the Bambino:

[Sc1yankee writes] Maybe Babe Ruth took the eighty-six-year jinx that he had put on the Red Sox and put it on NEW Yankee Stadium. Is it possible he is so mad they are not using the house that he built that he has put the eighty-six-year jinx on the new complex and the Yankees? I mean, let's look at the facts: (1) They open the new stadium with not just a loss, but a total embarrassing blow out (the old stadium was opened with a win over Boston); (2) Tex[Mark Teixeira] was a great hitter for eight years, comes here, and now he has a batting average that is close to .100; (3) CC [Sabathia] was dominating for the Brewers last season and carried them into the playoffs, [but] he can't even throw a strike in Yankee Stadium; (4) A-Rod doesn't notice he has a muscle tear in the off-season and misses the beginning of the 2009 season; (5) sealed files of 104 names of baseball players that tested positive for steroids, and the only name of 104 that comes out is A-Rod's . . . I don't know, you tell me, JINX or coincidence? Seems to me the old Babe is not happy about losing his home. Man, if he's this P.O.ed about the move, I'd hate to see what he is going to do when they tear down the "House That Ruth Built." He might increase the jinx to a hundred years instead of eighty-six![60]

[Mazin08 replies] Oh yeah . . . must be. Is Ruth why they failed to make the playoffs in the last year at the old Yankee Stadium? Guess he must have been mad that they were moving. Come on. The jinx is the Yankee greed.[61]

[Chongy replies] Ruth didn't jinx the Yankees, Steinbrenner did. The only time the Yankees got good was when he was gone. He was banned in the '70s for the Nixon campaign contributions and then in the '90s for the Winfield thing [Steinbrenner's attempts to discredit Yankee outfielder Dave Winfield] . . . For the goat, look no further.[62]

[Pal518 replies] Go ahead and move across the street. It may look like Yankee Stadium, it may have pictures of the greats, it may have all the bells and whistles, but it is not Yankee Stadium. So tear it down, but remember the Ghosts will stay home. Babe is not happy, so enjoy the next eighty-five years in the fake at 161 Street. The house that greed built.[63]

[RIEHL221 replies] Here we go. Another prophet making curses three games into the new stadium. Nostradumba$$.[64]

[Chongy replies] I'm a Yankee fan, but I believe they are indeed cursed. There are too many coincidences for it to be denied by me any longer. The Yankees were in Yankee Stadium for eighty-six years, the Red Sox were cursed for eighty-six years. Giuliani and Steinbrenner agreed to build a new stadium, on the taxpayer dime, in 2001. That World Series in 2001 was in the bag! Mariano [Rivera], Mr. Sandman, was closing it out, and then a Red Sox type collapse! A last bit of magic happened with Aaron Boone in 2003, but Florida owned the World Series in six games. Two thousand and four is undeniably the worst collapse in baseball history, at the hands of the Babe's former team. The last year in the old park the Yankees don't make the playoffs—wha wha WHAT? Opening series in this stadium, the Yankees are outscored forty to nineteen. Fenway was mortgaged on the Ruth trade and the Yankees sold him out to build their new stadium . . . The Babe was a working class guy and now working class guys can't afford to take the family to Yankee Stadium. For shame.[65]

And if suggestions of a new curse on the new Yankee Stadium impressed some as a rather faith-based criticism, some reality-based Yankee fans pondered a remedy for their team's woes which was firmly based in the material world—a return to the original Yankee Stadium:

[Retrokid writes] Not too late to move back in.[66]

[Close2the bats replies] Old Yankee Stadium is in no condition to play baseball in. There's no field. Two gaping holes in the outfield. It's too late.[67]

[Close2thebats writes] It's too bad they've already started dismantling the old one. They should have waited. This place has some kinks that need to be worked out! I bet if they went back to the old stadium there wouldn't be an empty seat in the house.[68]

[JackBauer4 replies] How DARE you criticize the $1.5 billion Boondoggle In The Bronx?!!!! These are the New York Yankees!!!! NO ONE questions THEM!!!!!!!![69]

[Danvid writes] This new place is just another fancy new ballpark with no feel and no emotion. What the heck was wrong with the old, original and ONLY Yankee Stadium?! I don't get good vibes about the House That George Built at all. Way to take the THE STADIUM, the freakin' cathedral of all baseball cathedrals, and ditch it for luxury suites and a hideous center field steak house.[70]

[06allstar replies] What was wrong with "old" Yankee Stadium? Not enough super boxes and suites. Unfortunately, that's the way it is now, so get used to it (and not just in NY). All the football stadiums look virtually alike. The arenas all look alike. And I agree—no emotion. I used to be able to watch hockey and basketball and you could just tell what arena they were in. Now, it's very depressing.[71]

It would be difficult to find a more succinct encapsulation of Yankee fan frustration with the new Yankee Stadium than 06allstar's directive that folks should just get used to something he finds very depressing. This vision of a great empire being exiled to house arrest in a palace of its own making has been seized upon by many Yankee fans, resulting in that peculiar sort of self-loathing that seems to plague empires struggling to maintain a history of greatness amid forces of change. Their dilemma might be seen as analogous to that of America at large, a preeminent nation in a world of less powerful competitors that often view their subordinate positions as a function of American dominance. In response to complaints about this arrangement from those less-favored nations, American opinion tends toward a bipolar split between those who would view such concerns as sour grapes over American success and those who would acknowledge some degree of American culpability. And faced with a global reality of increasing change and uncertainty, these positions tend to become hardened, with the "America first" crowd suggesting that others choose to "blame America first." Now, consider the Yankees to be that preeminent power in the world of baseball, and Yankee fans to be citizens of that powerful baseball nation. They possess a history of greatness, yet find themselves at a pause point which requires them to reconcile major changes to the status quo with the preservation of their legacy of dominance. Many will resolve this cognitive dissonance by strengthening their commitment to being even more loyal and unquestioning Yankee fans, but others will respond by directing their frustration and uncertainty inward through self-criticism. In other words, are those who see nothing but problems, deficiencies, and the loss of a cherished legacy resulting from the construction of a new Yankee Stadium "blaming the Yankees first"? Has the new Yankee Stadium precipitated a loyalty test within Yankee fandom, creating an irrevocable split between those who dare to question their leadership and those who shut up, pay up, and just get used to it?

Probably not. While initial reaction to the new Yankee Stadium tended to be a discussion featuring the passions of "loyal soldiers" and the "blame the Yankees first" crowd, a critical mass of Yankee fans occupied an ambivalent position best characterized as a "wait and see" attitude:

[Vivjeter writes] Well, I think this is a bittersweet home opener for a lot of Yankee fans. We will miss the tradition of old Yankee Stadium. However, even though it is gone it will not be forgotten. Some great names played there: Ruth, Gehrig, Dimaggio, Mantle, Yogi [Berra], to name a few. Add into that Paul [O'Neill], Bernie [Williams], Jeter, Mo [Mariano Rivera], Tino [Martinez] and Andy [Pettitte] among the more current players. As we pass down the accomplishments of these players, it will help keep alive the memories of old Yankee Stadium. In trying to be optimistic, New Yankee Stadium +New Season = Start of a NEW YANKEES DYNASTY.[72]

[Paleale13 writes] Don't get me wrong, it looks like an amazing stadium with the great hall, the resemblances of the original stadium, and everything else it has. But I already feel something is missing. I am more curious than excited to see the place. I guess I just have so many memories in the old place. It's almost like being forced out of your home that you grew up and lived in your whole life.[73]

[44IN77 writes] I agree. I had no problem with the old place. But as for tradition, even the original went through some major modifications in the '70s. "Good vibes" follow from great on-field moments and winning teams. Like a good steak, the new place just needs a little seasoning.[74]

[Celtsoxnyg writes] When a team leaves a place with a lot of history, it takes a while for the new place to have any meaning. I never thought the current home of the Celtics could compare with the old Boston Garden, and it took a while, but it's got that "feeling" to it now.[75]

Vivjeter's characterization of the Yankees' 2009 home opener as "bitter-sweet" may simply be taken as evidence of a mature acceptance of a new reality which doesn't necessarily erase past glory. For many who have witnessed those past glories, it is now an essential task that some avenue of inclusion be found for a new Yankee Stadium which, for better or worse, will now be an integral part of their project of fandom. Frank Revitt, one of those expatriate Yankee fans living in the Pocono Mountains of Pennsylvania, was trying his best to achieve that task on opening day. Admitting that he's "old enough to remember the old stadium before they remodeled in the '70s," Revitt deftly constructed a meaningful place for the new Yankee Stadium within his memories by claiming it evokes thoughts of "how the stadium was before. It's a new old stadium with modern amenities."[76] Part of Revitt's personal history as a Yankee fan was his status as a season ticket holder at the old Yankee Stadium, a status that he and his friends were forced to downscale due to the new and more costly pricing regime. Citing a price tag of $13,000 for the pair of lesser season tickets they purchased for the new Yankee Stadium's inaugural season, Revitt confessed that "it's an expensive habit but it's better than doing drugs, I guess."[77] Well, in terms of its effect on the state of one's general health, it may be better. But in terms of its centrality to one's existence, it may not be all that different. For many dedicated Yankee fans, issues of cost, obstructed views, and hideous center field steak houses are, ultimately, secondary concerns. New or old, Yankee Stadium is to Yankee fans as drugs are to the addict. In both cases, they need a fix just to get through the day.

NOTES

CHAPTER 1

1. Gustave Le Bon, *The Crowd: A Study of the Popular Mind* (New York: Viking Press, 1960; repr., New York: Penguin, 1977), 27. Citations are from the Penguin edition.

2. Ibid., 26.

3. Allen Guttmann, *Sport Spectators* (New York: Columbia University Press, 1986), 149.

4. Pierre Bourdieu, *Distinction: A Social Critique of the Judgement of Taste* (London: Routledge, 1984), 282.

5. Henry Jenkins, *Textual Poachers: Television Fans and Participatory Cultures* (London: Routledge, 1992), 284.

6. John Fiske, *Understanding Popular Culture* (Boston: Unwin and Hyman, 1989; repr., London: Routledge, 1991), 47. Citations are from the Routledge edition.

7. Melanie Klein, "Notes on Some Schizoid Mechanisms," in *Identity: A Reader*, eds. Paul Du Gay, Jessica Evans, and Peter Redman (London: Sage, 2000), 130–43.

8. Daniel Wann and others, *Sport Fans: the Psychology and Social Impact of Spectators* (New York: Routledge, 2001), 168.

9. Robert Cialdini and others, "Basking in Reflected Glory: Three (Football) Field Studies," *Journal of Personality and Social Psychology* 34 (1976): 366–75.

10. Wann and others, *Sport Fans*, 171–72.

11. Ibid., 176.

12. John Tulloch and Henry Jenkins, *Science Fiction Audiences: Watching "Doctor Who" and "Star Trek"* (London: Routledge, 1995), 149.

13. Matthew Hills, *Fan Cultures* (London: Routledge, 2002), 56–57.

14. Henry Jenkins, "Do You Enjoy Making the Rest of Us Feel Stupid?: alt. tv.twinpeaks, the Trickster Author, and Viewer Mastery," in *Fans, Bloggers, and Gamers: Exploring Participatory Culture* (New York: New York University Press, 2006), 117–18.

15. Adam N. Joinson, "Self-Disclosure in Computer-Mediated Communication: The Role of Self-Awareness and Visual Autonomy," *European Journal of Social Psychology* 31, no. 2 (2001): 177–92.

16. Katelyn Y. A. McKenna and John Bargh, "Coming Out in the Age of the Internet: Identity Demarginalization through Virtual Group Participation," *Journal of Personality and Social Psychology* 75, no. 3 (1998): 682.

17. Hills, *Fan Cultures*, 177.

18. Repsort, e-mail to Texas Rangers Fan Forum Message Boards, June 10, 2008, http://www.forums.mlb.com/ml-rangers.

19. Xyzybaluba, e-mail to Texas Rangers Fan Forum Message Boards, June 10, 2008, http://www.forums.mlb.com/ml-rangers.

20. Mike E, e-mail to Texas Rangers Fan Forum Message Boards, June 10, 2008, http://www.forums.mlb.com/ml-rangers.

21. Purpledog, e-mail to Texas Rangers Fan Forum Message Boards, June 10, 2008, http://www.forums.mlb.com/ml-rangers.

22. Cpt.ranger, e-mail to Texas Rangers Fan Forum Message Boards, June 11, 2008, http://www.forums.mlb.com/ml-rangers.

23. Hills, *Fan Cultures*, 66.

CHAPTER 2

1. Baseball Reference.com, http://www.baseball-reference.com/h/holtzke01.shtml (Ken Holtzman Statistics; accessed September 12, 2008).

2. Baseball Reference.com, http://www.baseball-reference.com/j/jacksre01.shtml (Reggie Jackson Statistics; accessed September 12, 2008).

3. Baseball Reference.com, http://www.baseball-reference.com/h/hunterca01.shtml (Catfish Hunter Statistics; accessed September 12, 2008).

4. Sweegger, e-mail to Oakland Athletics Fan Forum Message Boards, June 10, 2008, http://www.forums.mlb.com/ml-athletics.

5. Salbando6, e-mail to Oakland Athletics Fan Forum Message Boards, June 11, 2008, http://www.forums.mlb.com/ml-athletics.

6. Sweegger, e-mail to Oakland Athletics Fan Forum Message Boards, June 12, 2008, http://www.forums.mlb.com/ml-athletics.

7. Salbando6, e-mail to Oakland Athletics Fan Forum Message Boards, June 12, 2008, http://www.forums.mlb.com/ml-athletics.

8. Hills, *Fan Cultures*, 81.

9. Cornell Sandvoss, *Fans: The Meaning of Consumption* (Cambridge, UK: Polity, 2005), 112.

10. Ibid.

11. Pliny, *Letters*, trans. Betty Radice (Harmondsworth, UK: Penguin, 1963), 236.

12. No. 1baxfan, e-mail to Arizona Diamondbacks Fan Forum Message Boards, June 11, 2008, http://www.forums.mlb.com/ml-diamondbacks.

13. Natsfan11, e-mail to Washington Nationals Fan Forum Message Boards, June 11, 2008, http://www.forums.mlb.com/ml-washington.

14. BaseballReference.com, http://www.baseball-reference.com/d/damonjo01.shtml (Johnny Damon Statistics; accessed September 18, 2008).

15. Chgophil, e-mail to Chicago White Sox Fan Forum Message Boards, June 10, 2008, http://www.forums.mlb.com/ml-whitesox.

16. Baseball Reference.com, http://www.baseball-reference.com/g/gordoto01.shtml (Tom Gordon Statistics; accessed September 18, 2008).

17. Blu4evr, e-mail to Kansas City Royals Fan Forum Message Boards, June 10, 2008, http://www.forums.mlb.com/ml-royals.

18. Mattmel17, e-mail to Pittsburgh Pirates Fan Forum Message Boards, June 13, 2008, http://www.forums.mlb.com/ml-pirates.

19. Datsyuk13, e-mail to Detroit Tigers Fan Forum Message Boards, June 10, 2008, http://www.forums.mlb.com/ml-tigers.

20. Travelingmsfan1, e-mail to Chicago White Sox Fan Forum Message Boards, June 10, 2008, http://www.forums.mlb.com/ml-whitesox.

21. Chgophil, e-mail to Chicago White Sox Fan Forum Message Boards, June 10, 2008, http://www.forums.mlb.com/ml-whitesox.

22. Chopinchip, e-mail to Atlanta Braves Fan Forum Message Boards, June 10, 2008, http://www.forums.mlb.com/ml-braves.

23. Jaysfan, e-mail to Toronto Blue Jays Fan Forum Message Boards, June 10, 2008, http://www.forums.mlb.com/ml-bluejays.

24. JoeyEuclid, e-mail to Cleveland Indians Fan Forum Message Boards, June 11, 2008, http://www.forums.mlb.com/ml-indians.

25. Baseball Almanac.com, http://www.baseball-almanac.com/players/player.php?p=chapmra01 (Ray Chapman Baseball Stats; accessed September 23, 2008).

26. *New York Times*, "Beaned by a Pitch, Ray Chapman Dies," August 17, 1920, http://www.nytimes.com/packages/html/sports/year_in_sports/08.17.html.

27. Baseball Reference.com, http://baseball-reference.com/s/scorehe01.shtml (Herb Score Statistics; accessed September 25, 2008).

28. Prinalgin, "Herb Score—'If There is a Doctor in the Stands . . .'," *Associated Content*, August 21, 2006, http://associatedcontent.com/article/52315/herb_scoreif_there_is_a_doctor_in_the.html?cat=14.

29. Dean A. Sullivan, *Late Innings: A Documentary History of Baseball, 1945–1972* (Lincoln: University of Nebraska Press, 2002), 108.

30. BaseballReference.com, http://baseball-reference.com/bullpen/Herb_Score (Herb Score—BR Bullpen; accessed September 25, 2008).

31. Grammoxox, e-mail to Arizona Diamondbacks Fan Forum Message Boards, June 12, 2008, http://www.forums.mlb.com/ml-diamondbacks.

32. Theroostah, e-mail to Boston Red Sox Fan Forum Message Boards, June 10, 2008, http://www.forums.mlb.com/ml-redsox.

33. 3bwright, e-mail to New York Mets Fan Forum Message Boards, June 10, 2008, http://www.forums.mlb.com/ml-mets.

34. TS20, e-mail to Cincinnati Reds Fan Forum Message Boards, June 10, 2008, http://www.forums.mlb.com/ml-reds.

35. HolyCanoli, e-mail to Cincinnati Reds Fan Forum Message Boards, June 10, 2008, http://www.forums.mlb.com/ml-reds.

36. Bfos, e-mail to Kansas City Royals Fan Forum Message Boards, June 10, 2008, http://www.forums.mlb.com/ml-royals.

37. Blu4evr, email to Kansas City Royals Fan Forum Message Boards, June 10, 2008, http://www.forums.mlb.com/ml-royals.

38. Srs5020, e-mail to Pittsburgh Pirates Fan Forum Message Boards, June 10, 2008, http://www.forums.mlb.com/ml-pirates.

39. Baseball Chronology.com, http://www.baseballchronology.com/Baseball/Teams/Oakland (Oakland Athletics History; accessed January 5, 2009).

CHAPTER 3

1. Arkymark, e-mail to Washington Nationals Fan Forum Message Boards, June 10, 2008, http://www.forums.mlb.com/ml-washington.

2. 2run homer, e-mail to Atlanta Braves Fan Forum Message Boards, June 10, 2008, http://www.forums.mlb.com/ml-braves.

3. Abrave1, e-mail to Atlanta Braves Fan Forum Message Boards, June 10, 2008, http://www.forums.mlb.com/ml-braves.

4. Cowhide, e-mail to Kansas City Royals Fan Forum Message Boards, June 10, 2008, http://www.forums.mlb.com/ml-royals.

5. Baseball Almanac, http://www.baseball-almanac.com/boxscore/07241983.shtml (George Brett Pine Tar Game Enhanced Box Score; accessed November 19, 2008).

6. Metman79, e-mail to New York Mets Fan Forum Message Boards, June 10, 2008, http://www.forums.mlb.com/ml-mets.

7. The Baseball Page.com, http://www.thebaseballpage.com/players/stengca01.php (Casey Stengel; accessed November 20, 2008).

8. ABryant, e-mail to Washington Nationals Fan Forum Message Boards, June 10, 2008, http://www.forums.mlb.com/ml-washington.

9. Ericp331, e-mail to Washington Nationals Fan Forum Message Boards, June 10, 2008, http://www.forums.mlb.com/ml-washington.

10. Jon Heyman, "Fall Guy: Latest October Debacle Likely to End Torre's Tenure," *Sports Illustrated*, October 9, 2007, http://sportsillustrated.cnn.com/2007/writers/jon_heyman/10/09/scoop.tuesday/index.html.

11. "Torre Turns Down Offer to Return as Yanks' Skipper," *ESPN.com*, October 19, 2007, http://sports.espn.go.com/mlb/news/story?id=3069115.

12. Mark Feinsand, "Joe Torre Knocks Hank Steinbrenner on HBO's 'Real Sports,'" *New York Daily News*, October 24, 2007, http://www.nydailynews.com/sports/baseball/yankees/2007/10/24/2007–10–24_joe_torre_knocks_hank_stein brenner_on_hb.html.

13. Heyman, "Fall Guy."

14. Spastic, e-mail to Atlanta Braves Fan Forum Message Boards, June 10, 2008, http://www.forums.mlb.com/ml-braves.

15. Wsoxrock, e-mail to Chicago White Sox Fan Forum Message Boards, June 10, 2008, http://www.forums.mlb.com/ml-whitesox.

16. Chgophil, e-mail to Chicago White Sox Fan Forum Message Boards, June 10, 2008, http://www.forums.mlb.com/ml-whitesox.

17. Baseball-Reference.com, http://www.baseball-reference.com/r/ruthba01.shtml (Babe Ruth Statistics; accessed November 24, 2008).

18. Bruce Lowitt, "Bambino's Curse Begins as Red Sox Trade Ruth," *St. Petersburg (FL) Times*, December 21, 1999, http://www.sptimes.com/News/122199/Sports/Bambino_s_curse_begin.shtml.

19. Ibid.

20. Roger Dorn, e-mail to Cleveland Indians Fan Forum Message Boards, June 10, 2008, http://www.forums.mlb.com/ml-indians.

21. Freejamsociety, e-mail to Colorado Rockies Fan Forum Message Boards, June 10, 2008, http://www.forums.mlb.com/ml-rockies.

22. Schwender7, e-mail to Baltimore Orioles Fan Forum Message Boards, June 10, 2008, http://www.forums.mlb.com/ml-orioles.

23. Jcballer, e-mail to Philadelphia Phillies Fan Forum Message Boards, June 10, 2008, http://www.forums.mlb.com/ml-phillies.

24. CalifCajun, e-mail to Los Angeles Angels of Anaheim Fan Forum Message Boards, June 10, 2008, http://www.forums.mlb.com/ml-angels.

25. Cpt Jack, e-mail to Pittsburgh Pirates Fan Forum Message Boards, June 10, 2008, http://www.forums.mlb.com/ml-pirates.

26. Fla pirate, e-mail to Pittsburgh Pirates Fan Forum Message Boards, June 10, 2008, http://www.forums.mlb.com/ml-pirates.

27. Cpt Jack, e-mail to Pittsburgh Pirates Fan Forum Message Boards, June 10, 2008, http://www.forums.mlb.com/ml-pirates.

28. Accuscore, e-mail to Pittsburgh Pirates Fan Forum Message Boards, June 10, 2008, http://www.forums.mlb.com/ml-pirates.

29. Cecenation, e-mail to Pittsburgh Pirates Fan Forum Message Boards, June 10, 2008, http://www.forums.mlb.com/ml-pirates.

30. Cpt Jack, e-mail to Pittsburgh Pirates Fan Forum Message Boards, June 14, 2008, http://www.forums.mlb.com/ml-pirates.

31. Mongoose, e-mail to Pittsburgh Pirates Fan Forum Message Boards, June 15, 2008, http://www.forums.mlb.com/ml-pirates.

32. Yanksfan53, e-mail to Cleveland Indians Fan Forum Message Boards, June 10, 2008, http://www.forums.mlb.com/ml-indians.

33. Roger Dorn, e-mail to Cleveland Indians Fan Forum Message Boards, June 10, 2008, http://www.forums.mlb.com/ml-indians.

34. Yanksfan53, e-mail to Cleveland Indians Fan Forum Message Boards, June 10, 2008, http://www.forums.mlb.com/ml-indians.

35. Red 1, e-mail to Cleveland Indians Fan Forum Message Boards, June 10, 2008, http://www.forums.mlb.com/ml-indians.

36. Raptorman, e-mail to Oakland Athletics Fan Forum Message Boards, June 11, 2008, http://www.forums.mlb.com/ml-athletics.

37. Salbando6, e-mail to Oakland Athletics Fan Forum Message Boards, June 11, 2008, http://www.forums.mlb.com/ml-athletics.

38. Raptorman, e-mail to Oakland Athletics Fan Forum Message Boards, June 12, 2008, http://www.forums.mlb.com/ml-athletics.

39. Ericp331, e-mail to Washington Nationals Fan Forum Message Boards, June 10, 2008, http://www.forums.mlb.com/ml-washington.

40. RayD, e-mail to Washington Nationals Fan Forum Message Boards, June 10, 2008, http://www.forums.mlb.com/ml-washington.

41. Official Site of the New York Yankees, http://newyork.yankees.mlb.com/nyy/history/timeline3.jsp (Yankees Timeline; accessed December 2, 2008).

42. Stefan Szymanski and Andrew S. Zimbalist, *National Pastime: How Americans Play Baseball and the Rest of the World Plays Soccer* (Washington, DC: Brookings Institution Press, 2005), 149.

43. Trademarc1, e-mail to Chicago White Sox Fan Forum Message Boards, June 10, 2008, http://www.forums.mlb.com/ml-whitesox.

44. Baseball Chronology, http://www.baseballchronology.com/Baseball/Teams/New_York_Yankees/ (New York Yankees History; accessed December 4, 2008).

45. Szymanski and Zimbalist, *National Pastime*, 148.

46. Chgophil, e-mail to Chicago White Sox Fan Forum Message Boards, June 10, 2008, http://www.forums.mlb.com/ml-whitesox.

47. Zilla2005, e-mail to Washington Nationals Fan Forum Message Boards, June 10, 2008, http://www.forums.mlb.com/ml-washington.

48. Ericp331, e-mail to Washington Nationals Fan Forum Message Boards, June 10, 2008, http://www.forums.mlb.com/ml-washington.

49. Jono3, e-mail to Chicago Cubs Fan Forum Message Boards, June 10, 2008, http://www.forums.mlb.com/ml-cubs.

50. Rds1, e-mail to Los Angeles Angels of Anaheim Fan Forum Message Boards, June 10, 2008, http://www.forums.mlb.com/ml-angels.

51. Sirphobos, e-mail to St. Louis Cardinals Fan Forum Message Boards, June 10, 2008, http://www.forums.mlb.com/ml-cardinals.

52. Hess, e-mail to St. Louis Cardinals Fan Forum Message Boards, June 10, 2008, http://www.forums.mlb.com/ml-cardinals.

53. Joe Queenan, *True Believers: The Tragic Inner Life of Sports Fans* (New York: Henry Holt, 2003), 49–50.

54. Ibid., 51.

55. NYCanito, e-mail to Florida Marlins Fan Forum Message Boards, June 10, 2008, http://www.forums.mlb.com/ml-marlins.

56. Theroostah, e-mail to Boston Red Sox Fan Forum Message Boards, June 12, 2008, http://www.forums.mlb.com/ml-redsox.

57. Fla pirate, e-mail to Pittsburgh Pirates Fan Forum Message Boards, June 10, 2008, http://www.forums.mlb.com/ml-pirates.

58. BeerMan58, e-mail to Chicago White Sox Fan Forum Message Boards, June 10, 2008, http://www.forums.mlb.com/ml-whitesox.

59. Doc hamp, e-mail to Pittsburgh Pirates Fan Forum Message Boards, June 10, 2008, http://www.forums.mlb.com/ml-pirates.

60. Srs5020, e-mail to Pittsburgh Pirates Fan Forum Message Boards, June 10, 2008, http://www.forums.mlb.com/ml-pirates.

61. Movelli, e-mail to Chicago Cubs Fan Forum Message Boards, June 10, 2008, http://www.forums.mlb.com/ml-cubs.

62. Cpt Jack, e-mail to Pittsburgh Pirates Fan Forum Message Boards, June 10, 2008, http://www.forums.mlb.com/ml-pirates.

63. Accuscore, e-mail to Pittsburgh Pirates Fan Forum Message Boards, June 10, 2008, http://www.forums.mlb.com/ml-pirates.

64. Szymanski and Zimbalist, *National Pastime*, 153.

65. Cpt Jack, e-mail to Pittsburgh Pirates Fan Forum Message Boards, June 11, 2008, http://www.forums.mlb.com/ml-pirates.

66. Upncoming, e-mail to Tampa Bay Rays Fan Forum Message Boards, June 10, 2008, http://www.forums.mlb.com/ml-rays.

67. 21sthebest, e-mail to Pittsburgh Pirates Fan Forum Message Boards, June 10, 2008, http://www.forums.mlb.com/ml-pirates.

68. Ben29, e-mail to Philadelphia Phillies Fan Forum Message Boards, June 10, 2008, http://www.forums.mlb.com/ml-phillies.

69. TS20, e-mail to Cincinnati Reds Fan Forum Message Boards, June 10, 2008, http://www.forums.mlb.com/ml-reds.

70. Bossk, e-mail to San Diego Padres Fan Forum Message Boards, June 10, 2008, http://www.forums.mlb.com/ml-padres.

CHAPTER 4

1. Prashant Gopal, "Where Would You Relocate for a Job?" *Business Week*, November 20, 2008, http://www.businessweek.com/lifestyle/content/nov2008/bw20081120_631419.htm.

2. Doc hamp, e-mail to Pittsburgh Pirates Fan Forum Message Boards, June 10, 2008, http://www.forums.mlb.com/ml-pirates.

3. SarBear, e-mail to Arizona Diamondbacks Fan Forum Message Boards, June 10, 2008, http://www.forums.mlb.com/ml-diamondbacks.

4. DeronJ, e-mail to Cincinnati Reds Fan Forum Message Boards, June 10, 2008, http://www.forums.mlb.com/ml-reds.

5. Kidoist, e-mail to Detroit Tigers Fan Forum Message Boards, June 10, 2008, http://www.forums.mlb.com/ml-tigers.

6. Bizz12, e-mail to Arizona Diamondbacks Fan Forum Message Boards, June 10, 2008, http://www.forums.mlb.com/ml-diamondbacks.

7. Elek5, e-mail to Florida Marlins Fan Forum Message Boards, June 11, 2008, http://www.forums.mlb.com/ml-marlins.

8. Yankeesvictory, e-mail to Colorado Rockies Fan Forum Message Boards, June 10, 2008, http://www.forums.mlb.com/ml-rockies.

9. AdRock18, e-mail to New York Mets Fan Forum Message Boards, June 10, 2008, http://www.forums.mlb.com/ml-mets.

10. Theroostah, e-mail to Boston Red Sox Fan Forum Message Boards, June 10, 2008, http://www.forums.mlb.com/ml-redsox.

11. Fargol, e-mail to New York Mets Fan Forum Message Boards, June 10, 2008, http://www.forums.mlb.com/ml-mets.

12. Elek5, e-mail to Florida Marlins Fan Forum Message Boards, June 11, 2008, http://www.forums.mlb.com/ml-marlins.

13. Queenan, *True Believers*, 8.

14. Green420, e-mail to Baltimore Orioles Fan Forum Message Boards, June 10, 2008, http://www.forums.mlb.com/ml-orioles.

15. Elek5, e-mail to Florida Marlins Fan Forum Message Boards, June 11, 2008, http://www.forums.mlb.com/ml-marlins.

16. Upncoming, e-mail to Tampa Bay Rays Fan Forum Message Boards, June 10, 2008, http://www.forums.mlb.com/ml-rays.

17. Chgophil, e-mail to Chicago White Sox Fan Forum Message Boards, June 10, 2008, http://www.forums.mlb.com/ml-whitesox.

18. Will Blythe, *To Hate Like This Is to Be Happy Forever* (New York: Harper Collins, 2006), 4–5.

19. Poleymak, e-mail to Atlanta Braves Fan Forum Message Boards, June 10, 2008, http://www.forums.mlb.com/ml-braves.

20. Schwender7, e-mail to Baltimore Orioles Fan Forum Message Boards, June 10, 2008, http://www.forums.mlb.com/ml-orioles.

21. Daygloman2, e-mail to Los Angeles Angels of Anaheim Fan Forum Message Boards, June 10, 2008, http://www.forums.mlb.com/ml-angels.

22. Bill Simmons, "Congratulations for Being a Yankee Fan, LeBron," *ESPN Page 2*, October 10, 2007, http://sports.espn.go.com/espn/page2/story?page=simmons/071010.

23. Nhraysfan, e-mail to Tampa Bay Rays Fan Forum Message Boards, June 10, 2008, http://www.forums.mlb.com/ml-rays.

24. Wann and others, *Sport Fans*, 5.

25. Ibid., 7.

26. Garry Crawford, *Consuming Sport: Fans, Sport, and Culture* (London: Routledge, 2004), 59–60.

27. Goober21, e-mail to Pittsburgh Pirates Fan Forum Message Boards, June 10, 2008, http://www.forums.mlb.com/ml-pirates.

28. Sandvoss, *Fans*, 136.

29. Enjoybb, e-mail to Seattle Mariners Fan Forum Message Boards, June 10, 2008, http://www.forums.mlb.com/ml-mariners.

30. Natsfan11, e-mail to Washington Nationals Fan Forum Message Boards, June 11, 2008, http://www.forums.mlb.com/ml-washington.

31. Queenan, *True Believers*, 75.

CHAPTER 5

1. Bizz12, e-mail to Arizona Diamondbacks Fan Forum Message Boards, June 10, 2008, http://www.forums.mlb.com/ml-diamondbacks.

2. SarBear, e-mail to Arizona Diamondbacks Fan Forum Message Boards, June 10, 2008, http://www.forums.mlb.com/ml-diamondbacks.

3. Dbaxpwnall, e-mail to Arizona Diamondbacks Fan Forum Message Boards, June 12, 2008, http://www.forums.mlb.com/ml-diamondbacks.

4. Schwender7, e-mail to Baltimore Orioles Fan Forum Message Boards, June 10, 2008, http://www.forums.mlb.com/ml-orioles.

5. Willym, e-mail to Baltimore Orioles Fan Forum Message Boards, June 10, 2008, http://www.forums.mlb.com/ml-orioles.

6. Lynnrd, e-mail to Baltimore Orioles Fan Forum Message Boards, June 10, 2008, http://www.forums.mlb.com/ml-orioles.

7. Baseball Chronology, http://www.baseballchronolgy.com/Baseball/Teams/New_York_Yankees/ (New York Yankees History; accessed January 13, 2009).

8. Travelingmsfan1, e-mail to Chicago White Sox Fan Forum Message Boards, June 10, 2008, http://www.forums.mlb.com/ml-whitesox.

9. Michael Costello, "Politically Correct Heckling," *The Pajamahadin*, May 16, 2002, http://michaelcostello.blogspot.com/2002_05_01_archive.html.

10. Lynnrd, e-mail to Baltimore Orioles Fan Forum Message Boards, June 11, 2008, http://www.forums.mlb.com/ml-orioles.

11. Thelocal9, e-mail to Philadelphia Phillies Fan Forum Message Boards, June 10, 2008, http://www.forums.mlb.com/ml-phillies.

12. Wann and others, *Sport Fans*, 5.

13. Arkymark, e-mail to Washington Nationals Fan Forum Message Boards, June 11, 2008, http://www.forums.mlb.com/ml-washington.

14. Gophils412, e-mail to Philadelphia Phillies Fan Forum Message Boards, June 10, 2008, http://www.forums.mlb.com/ml-phillies.

15. Tigro, e-mail to Arizona Diamondbacks Fan Forum Message Boards, June 12, 2008, http://www.forums.mlb.com/ml-diamondbacks.

16. Jerseygirl, e-mail to St. Louis Cardinals Fan Forum Message Boards, June 10, 2008, http://www.forums.mlb.com/ml-cardinals.

17. Dukeofurl, e-mail to St. Louis Cardinals Fan Forum Message Boards, June 10, 2008, http://www.forums.mlb.com/ml-cardinals.

18. Maui4birds, e-mail to Baltimore Orioles Fan Forum Message Boards, June 10, 2008, http://www.forums.mlb.com/ml-orioles.

19. Johnny u, e-mail to Cincinnati Reds Fan Forum Message Boards, June 10, 2008, http://www.forums.mlb.com/ml-reds.

20. Natsfan11, e-mail to Washington Nationals Fan Forum Message Boards, June 11, 2008, http://www.forums.mlb.com/ml-washington.

21. GnatsFan, e-mail to Baltimore Orioles Fan Forum Message Boards, June 10, 2008, http://www,forums.mlb.com/ml-orioles.

22. El_Guapo, e-mail to New York Mets Fan Forum Message Boards, June 10, 2008, http://www.forums.mlb.com/ml-mets.

23. RedSoxinVt, e-mail to Philadelphia Phillies Fan Forum Message Boards, June 10, 2008, http://www.forums.mlb.com/ml-phillies.

24. S FL Gio, e-mail to Boston Red Sox Fan Forum Message Boards, June 11, 2008, http://forums.mlb.com/ml-redsox.

25. Poleymak, e-mail to Atlanta Braves Fan Forum Message Boards, June 10, 2008, http://www.forums.mlb.com/ml-braves.

26. Yanksfan53, e-mail to Detroit Tigers Fan Forum Message Boards, June 10, 2008, http://www.forums.mlb.com/ml-tigers.

27. Travon, e-mail to Los Angeles Angels of Anaheim Fan Forum Message Boards, June 10, 2008, http://www.forums.mlb.com/ml-angels.

28. Ramki, e-mail to St. Louis Cardinals Fan Forum Message Boards, June 10, 2008, http://www.forums.mlb.com/ml-cardinals.

29. William Hazlitt, *On the Pleasure of Hating* (New York: Penguin, 2005), 105.

30. Blu4evr, e-mail to Kansas City Royals Fan Forum Message Boards, June 10, 2008, http://www.forums.mlb.com/ml-royals.

31. Ogredsfan, e-mail to Cincinnati Reds Fan Forum Message Boards, June 10, 2008, http://www.forums.mlb.com/ml-reds.

32. David Byrne, "Heaven," copyright Index Music/Bleu Disque Music, 1979.

33. Hazlitt, *On the Pleasure of Hating*, 106.

34. Salbando6, e-mail to Oakland Athletics Fan Forum Message Boards, June 12, 2008, http://www.forums.mlb.com/ml-athletics.

35. Ty mccobb, e-mail to Detroit Tigers Fan Forum Message Boards, June 10, 2008, http://www.forums.mlb.com/ml-tigers.

36. Hazlitt, *On the Pleasure of Hating*, 104.

37. Mojo32, e-mail to Arizona Diamondbacks Fan Forum Message Boards, June 12, 2008, http://www.forums.mlb.com/ml-diamondbacks.

CHAPTER 6

1. D. W. Winnicott, *Playing and Reality* (London: Tavistock, 1971), 1–25.

2. Hills, *Fan Cultures*, 105–6.

3. Ibid., 108.

4. Ibid., 109.

5. Ibid., 111.

6. Wann and others, *Sport Fans*, 60.

7. Winnicott, *Playing and Reality*, 3.

8. Ibid., 14.

9. Sandvoss, *Fans*, 92.

10. Ibid., 104.

11. Ibid., 112.

12. Ibid., 64.

13. Ibid.

14. Crawford, *Consuming Sport*, 59.

15. Ibid., 158–60.

16. Sandvoss, *Fans*, 64.

17. Roger Aden, *Popular Stories and Promised Lands: Fan Culture and Symbolic Pilgrimages* (Tuscaloosa: University of Alabama Press, 1999), 93.

18. Hills, *Fan Cultures*, 146.

19. Ibid., 153–54.

20. Ibid., 154.

21. Nicholas Abercrombie and Brian Longhurst, *Audiences: A Sociological Theory of Performance and Imagination* (London: Sage, 1998), 131–39.

22. Sandvoss, *Fans*, 125.

23. Ibid., 126.

24. Ibid., 137.

25. Sigmund Freud, *Group Psychology and the Analysis of the Ego*, trans. and ed. James Strachey (New York: Norton, 1959), 33.

26. Ballparks of Baseball, http://www.ballparksofbaseball.com/al/YankeeSta diumII.htm (Ballparks of Baseball-Yankee Stadium-New York Yankees; accessed February 18, 2009).

27. Official Site of the New York Yankees, http://www.newyork.yankees. mlb.com/nyy/ballpark/new_stadium_comparison.jsp (New Yankee Stadium Comparison; accessed February 18, 2009).

28. "Seats Behind Home Plate at the Yankees New Stadium Cost $500–$2500," *ESPN.com*, March 21, 2008, http://sports.espn.go.com/mlb/news/story? id=3305979.

29. Russell Goldman, "For Those Who Can Afford It, Yankees Sell Tickets for $2,500," *ABC News*, March 25, 2008, http://abcnews.go.com/Sports/Story? id=4515520&page=2.

30. Jerry Crasnick, "Yankees Acquire Swisher, Send Betemit and Two Pitchers to White Sox," *ESPN.com*, November 13, 2008, http://sports.espn.go.com/mlb /news/story?id=3700869.

31. Tyler Kepner, "Burnett and Yankees Reach 5-Year Deal," *New York Times*, December 12, 2008, http://www.nytimes.com/2008/12/13/sports/baseball/ 13yanks.html.

32. Buster Olney, "Sources: 'Tex' Takes Yanks' 8-Year Deal," *ESPN.com*, December 23, 2008, http://sports.espn.go.com/mlb/news/story?id=3790141.

33. Ibid.

34. Buster Olney, "Winners and Losers from Yanks' Signing of Teixeira," *ESPN.com*, December 24, 2008, http://sports.espn.go.com/espn/blog/index?entry ID=3791485&name=olney_buster.

EPILOGUE

1. Denise Smithson, "Yankee Stadium New," *Betting for a Profit*, April 2, 2009, http://www.bettingenterprise.com/2009/04/02/yankee-stadium-new/.

2. Richard Sandomir, "Mayor's Stadium Plan is Grandly Vague, Experts Say," New York Times, January 16, 1999, http://www.nytimes.com/1999/01/16/ nyre gion/mayor-s-stadium-plan-is-grandly-vague-experts-say.html?sec=&spon.

3. Smithson, "Yankee Stadium New."

4. Steven Malanga, "How Not to Develop the Far West Side," *City Journal*, Spring 2005, http://www.city-journal.org/html/15_2_far_west_side.html.

5. "Yankee Stadium Proposal," *onNYTurf*, March 29, 2006, http://www.on nyturf.com/wiki/index.php?page=Yankee+Stadium+Proposal.

6. Ncyankfan7, e-mail to New York Yankees Fan Forum Message Boards, April 21, 2009, http://www.forums.mlb.com/ml-yankees.

7. Ryanation4, e-mail to New York Yankees Fan Forum Message Boards, April 21, 2009, http://www.forums.mlb.com/ml-yankees.

8. Shoveit6963, e-mail to New York Yankees Fan Forum Message Boards, April 21, 2009, http://www.forums.mlb.com/ml-yankees.

9. Stevem7, e-mail to New York Yankees Fan Forum Message Boards, April 16, 2009, http://www.forums.mlb.com/ml-yankees.

10. WoodyDee, e-mail to New York Yankees Fan Forum Message Boards, April 16, 2009, http://www.forums.mlb.com/ml-yankees.

11. MarisHOF, e-mail to New York Yankees Fan Forum Message Boards, April 18, 2009, http://www.forums.mlb.com/ml-yankees.

12. PridePowerPinstripes, e-mail to New York Yankees Fan Forum Message Boards, April 18, 2009, http://www.forums.mlb.com/ml-yankees.

13. MarisHOF, e-mail to New York Yankees Fan Forum Message Boards, April 18, 2009, http://www.forums.mlb.com/ml-yankees.

14. Okefanokie, e-mail to New York Yankees Fan Forum Message Boards, April 18, 2009, http://www.forums.mlb.com/ml-yankees.

15. Roywitefan, e-mail to New York Yankees Fan Forum Message Boards, April 18, 2009, http://www.forums.mlb.com/ml-yankees.

16. Portwa, e-mail to New York Yankees Fan Forum Message Boards, April 17, 2009, http://www.forums.mlb.com/ml-yankees.

17. 46fan4evr, e-mail to New York Yankees Fan Forum Message Boards, April 17, 2009, http://www.forums.mlb.com/ml-yankees.

18. RayG, e-mail to New York Yankees Fan Forum Message Boards, April 17, 2009, http://www.forums.mlb.com/ml-yankees.

19. Ruhikuz, e-mail to New York Yankees Fan Forum Message Boards, April 17, 2009, http://www.forums.mlb.com/ml-yankees.

20. 46fan4evr, e-mail to New York Yankees Fan Forum Message Boards, April 17, 2009, http://www.forums.mlb.com/ml-yankees.

21. 84yrs4_26, e-mail to New York Yankees Fan Forum Message Boards, April 20, 2009, http://www.forums.mlb.com/ml-yankees.

22. Riron, e-mail to New York Yankees Fan Forum Message Boards, April 20, 2009, http://www.forums.mlb.com/ml-yankees.

23. Stevem7, e-mail to New York Yankees Fan Forum Message Boards, April 20, 2009, http://www.forums.mlb.com/ml-yankees.

24. Babebomber, e-mail to New York Yankees Fan Forum Message Boards, April 20, 2009, http://www.forums.mlb.com/ml-yankees.

25. 62 nova, e-mail to New York Yankees Fan Forum Message Boards, April 20, 2009, http://www.forums.mlb.com/ml-yankees.

26. 9roger9, e-mail to New York Yankees Fan Forum Message Boards, April 20, 2009, http://www.forums.mlb.com/ml-yankees.

27. RayG, e-mail to New York Yankees Fan Forum Message Boards, April 20, 2009, http://www.forums.mlb.com/ml-yankees.

28. Joiseyank, e-mail to New York Yankees Fan Forum Message Boards, April 20, 2009, http://www.forums.mlb.com/ml-yankees.

29. MarisHOF, e-mail to New York Yankees Fan Forum Message Boards, April 20, 2009, http://www.forums.mlb.com/ml-yankees.

30. Sparkylyle, e-mail to New York Yankees Fan Forum Message Boards, April 20, 2009, http://www.forums.mlb.com/ml-yankees.

31. A-roddaman, e-mail to New York Yankees Fan Forum Message Boards, April 19, 2009, http://www.forums.mlb.com/ml-yankees.

32. Close2thebats, e-mail to New York Yankees Fan Forum Message Boards, April 19, 2009, http://www.forums.mlb.com/ml-yankees.

33. Pdxyankee1, e-mail to New York Yankees Fan Forum Message Boards, April 19, 2009, http://www.forums.mlb.com/ml-yankees.

34. A-roddaman, e-mail to New York Yankees Fan Forum Message Boards, April 19, 2009, http://www.forums.mlb.com/ml-yankees.

35. Ibid.

36. Danyeo, e-mail to New York Yankees Fan Forum Message Boards, April 19, 2009, http://www.forums.mlb.com/ml-yankees.

37. A-roddaman, e-mail to New York Yankees Fan Forum Message Boards, April 19, 2009, http://www.forums.mlb.com/ml-yankees.

38. 96champs, e-mail to New York Yankees Fan Forum Message Boards, April 20, 2009, http://www.forums.mlb.com/ml-yankees.

39. Scottwaz, e-mail to New York Yankees Fan Forum Message Boards, April 20, 2009, http://www.forums.mlb.com/ml-yankees.

40. RIEHL221, e-mail to New York Yankees Fan Forum Message Boards, April 20, 2009, http://www.forums.mlb.com/ml-yankees.

41. Scottwaz, e-mail to New York Yankees Fan Forum Message Boards, April 20, 2009, http://www.forums.mlb.com/ml-yankees.

42. Stevem7, e-mail to New York Yankees Fan Forum Message Boards, April 20, 2009, http://www.forums.mlb.com/ml-yankees.

43. 161curse, e-mail to New York Yankees Fan Forum Message Boards, April 21, 2009, http://www.forums.mlb.com/ml-yankees.

44. "Bob Sheppard to Miss Beginning of 2009 Season," *Official Site of the New York Yankees*, March 31, 2009, http://newyork.yankees.mlb.com/news/press_releases/press_release.jsp?ymd=20090331&content_id=4096258%vkey=pr_nyy&fext=.jsp&c_id=nyy.

45. Sgh07, e-mail to New York Yankees Fan Forum Message Boards, April 18, 2009, http://www.forums.mlb.com/ml-yankees.

46. Nyygal007, e-mail to New York Yankees Fan Forum Message Boards, April 21, 2009, http://www.forums.mlb.com/ml-yankees.

47. Okefanokie, e-mail to New York Yankees Fan Forum Message Boards, April 18, 2009, http://www.forums.mlb.com/ml-yankees.

48. Sgh07, e-mail to New York Yankees Fan Forum Message Boards, April 20, 2009, http://www.forums.mlb.com/ml-yankees.

49. Okefanokie, e-mail to New York Yankees Fan Forum Message Boards, April 21, 2009, http://www.forums.mlb.com/ml-yankees.

50. 46fan4evr, e-mail to New York Yankees Fan Forum Message Boards, April 21, 2009, http://www.forums.mlb.com/ml-yankees.

51. Ruhikuz, e-mail to New York Yankees Fan Forum Message Boards, April 21, 2009, http://www.forums.mlb.com/ml-yankees.

52. Nyygal007, e-mail to New York Yankees Fan Forum Message Boards, April 21, 2009, http://www.forums.mlb.com/ml-yankees.

53. HolyCanoli, e-mail to New York Yankees Fan Forum Message Boards, April 21, 2009, http://www.forums.mlb.com/ml-yankees.

54. 46fan4evr, e-mail to New York Yankees Fan Forum Message Boards, April 21, 2009, http://www.forums.mlb.com/ml-yankees.

55. DJmuggs, e-mail to New York Yankees Fan Forum Message Boards, April 18, 2009, http://www.forums.mlb.com/ml-yankees.

56. Redsox17, e-mail to New York Yankees Fan Forum Message Boards, April 19, 2009, http://www.forums.mlb.com/ml-yankees.

57. Ncyankfan7, e-mail to New York Yankees Fan Forum Message Boards, April 20, 2009, http://www.forums.mlb.com/ml-yankees.

58. 1927yankee, e-mail to New York Yankees Fan Forum Message Boards, April 16, 2009, http://www.forums.mlb.com/ml-yankees.

59. Sc1yankee, e-mail to New York Yankees Fan Forum Message Boards, April 16, 2009, http://www.forums.mlb.com/ml-yankees.

60. Ibid.

61. Mazin08, e-mail to New York Yankees Fan Forum Message Boards, April 16, 2009, http://www.forums.mlb.com/ml-yankees.

62. Chongy, e-mail to New York Yankees Fan Forum Message Boards, April 17, 2009, http://www.forums.mlb.com/ml-yankees.

63. Pal518, e-mail to New York Yankees Fan Forum Message Boards, April 18, 2009, http://www.forums.mlb.com/ml-yankees.

64. RIEHL221, e-mail to New York Yankees Fan Forum Message Boards, April 18, 2009, http://www.forums.mlb.com/ml-yankees.

65. Chongy, e-mail to New York Yankees Fan Forum Message Boards, April 19, 2009, http://www.forums.mlb.com/ml-yankees.

66. Retrokid, e-mail to New York Yankees Fan Forum Message Boards, April 19, 2009, http://www.forums.mlb.com/ml-yankees.

67. Close2thebats, e-mail to New York Yankees Fan Forum Message Boards, April 19, 2009, http://www.forums.mlb.com/ml-yankees.

68. Ibid.

69. JackBauer4, e-mail to New York Yankees Fan Forum Message Boards, April 19, 2009, http://www.forums.mlb.com/ml-yankees.

70. Danvid, e-mail to New York Yankees Fan Forum Message Boards, April 19, 2009, http://www,forums.mlb.com/ml-yankees.

71. 06allstar, e-mail to New York Yankees Fan Forum Message Boards, April 19, 2009, http://www.forums.mlb.com/ml-yankees.

72. Vivjeter, e-mail to New York Yankees Fan Forum Message Boards, April 16, 2009, http://www.forums.mlb.com/ml-yankees.

73. Paleale13, e-mail to New York Yankees Fan Forum Message Boards, April 16, 2009, http://www.forums.mlb.com/ml-yankees.

74. 44IN77, e-mail to New York Yankees Fan Forum Message Boards, April 19, 2009, http://www.forums.mlb.com/ml-yankees.

75. Celtsoxnyg, e-mail to New York Yankees Fan Forum Message Boards, April 20, 2009, http://www.forums.mlb.com/ml-yankees.

76. Marta Gouger, "Opening Day a Thrill for Yankee Fans," *Pocono Record*, April 17, 2009.

77. Ibid.

INDEX

About the Author

CHARLES R. WARNER holds a Ph.D. in American Culture Studies from Bowling Green State University and is currently a Professor of Communication Studies at East Stroudsburg University of Pennsylvania, where he teaches courses in media studies and popular culture. His scholarly interests focus on youth culture, popular entertainments, and consumption as a cultural practice. At this point in life, he is painfully aware that his window of opportunity for becoming the Cleveland Indians' second baseman is rapidly closing. Dr. Warner lives in East Stroudsburg, Pennsylvania, with his wife and daughter (both of whom are Yankee fans).